Your Baby's First Year

Your Baby's First Year

A Guide for Teenage Parents

Jeanne Warren Lindsay, MA, CFCS

Morning Glory Press

Buena Park, California

Your Baby's First Year
is part of a five-book series. Other titles are:

Your Pregnancy and Newborn Journey:
A Guide for Pregnant Teens

The Challenge of Toddlers:
Parenting Your Child from One to Three

Discipline from Birth to Three:
How Teen Parents Can Prevent and Deal
with Discipline Problems with Babies and Toddlers

Teen Dads: Rights, Responsibilities and Joys

Library of Congress Cataloging-in-Publication Data
Lindsay, Jeanne Warren.
    Your baby's first year : a guide for teenage parents / Jeanne
Warren Lindsay. -- Rev. ed.
        p.   cm. -- (Teens parenting)
    Includes bibliographical references (p.   ) and index.
    ISBN 1-885356-32-3 (hbk) -- ISBN 1-885356-33-1 (pbk.)
    1. Teenage parents--United States.   2. Child rearing--United
States.   3. Infants--United States.   I. Title.   II. Series:
Lindsay, Jeanne Warren.   Teens parenting.
HQ759.64.L57   1998
649'. 122--dc21   98-7746
                                                        CIP

MORNING GLORY PRESS, INC.
6595 San Haroldo Way   Buena Park, CA 90620-3748
714/828-1998   1/888-612-8254
Printed and bound in the United States of America

Contents

Preface

Nearly half a million teenagers deliver babies each year in the United States, and many of the fathers of these babies are also teenagers. Yet most parenting books are written as if all parents are adults.

A parent who is still an adolescent is part of two worlds, and these two worlds may be in conflict. A teenage parent's life is quite different from the lives of her/his non-parent peers. It may also be quite different from the young families who delay childbearing until both parents have completed their education and are able to form their own household.

I have worked with hundreds of pregnant and parenting teenagers during the past twenty-five years. Because our school district provides an infant center to care for their babies, many of these young mothers continue attending school on campus after they deliver. Many have fallen into parenthood accidentally, but it is no accident that many are good parents. They've had help along the way from their families and their community, and, most important, they work hard at their parenting job.

This book is a parenting guide especially designed for teenage parents. A major part of it are the comments and parenting suggestions from young people who are "practicing" parents, teenagers who have children of their own. Some are married, some are single. Whatever their marital status, they are more likely to have money problems than are older parents. Many live with their own parents because of their age and/or lack of money.

Names of parents, their children, and a few personal details have been changed in the quotes in order to protect confidentiality. Parents' and children's ages have not been changed. Their comments are real, and quotes are almost always in the exact words used by the young parent.

Your Baby's First Year is part of a five-book series for pregnant and parenting teens. Other titles are *Your Pregnancy and Newborn Journey* co-authored by Jean Brunelli, PHN, *Discipline from Birth to Three* co-authored by Sally McCullough, *The Challenge of Toddlers,* and *Teen Dads.*

Chapter 5 of *Your Baby's First Year* is written directly to teen fathers while chapter 6 focuses on the special needs of mothers who parent alone. The rest of the book applies both to single parents and to couples who are parenting together.

Parenting at 15, or even 17, is an extremely difficult task. In fact, parenting at any age is quite a challenge for most of us. I hope this book will help young parents understand a little better the world of babies during that all-important first year of parenting.

Jeanne Warren Lindsay   *June, 1998*

Foreword

I became a father for the first time at age 30. All three of my children are teenagers now. They are offering all of the parenting challenges that teens typically present. However, nothing has been more exciting, yet completely terrifying, than that first day we spent at home alone with our firstborn. It all seemed so easy while our family was surrounded by the caring, competent attention of the hospital staff. Their confidence inspired our own. Feeding, diapering, feeding again, consoling, diapering again, and sleeping all seemed so simple. We felt so together and so in control.

Then, we went home.

Almost immediately, the routine that seemed easy and normal in the hospital took on a life of its own. Without the support of the hospital staff, each of those tasks grew huge and loomed ominously over us. The feelings of control and competence we had felt in the hospital were revealed for what they were — mere illusions created by the euphoria of brand-new parenthood. We all knew we were in over our heads. Our son, frustrated by the failure of his parents to fully comprehend the meaning of his cries, only cried harder. His mother, still sore and recovering from the caesarian childbirth, joined him. Finally, succumbing to my own exhaustion and failure to achieve the same level of competence I had felt only a day before, I offered my voice to complete the trio of cries and sobs.

I realize now that first day alone as parents might not have been as terrifying if we'd had Jeanne Warren Lindsay's book, *Your Baby's First Year*. If I, as a 30-year-old father, had such difficulty adjusting to the new demands of parenting, how must it be for a teen mom or teen dad?

Jeanne knows the answer to this question better than anyone else I know. Drawing upon her years of working with teen parents and her own experience as a mother, she now offers this updated version of *Your Baby's First Year*. Written specifically to teen parents, it nonetheless provides practical, insightful information for all parents of newborns. Jeanne's love for and belief in teen moms and dads comes through page after page. From the easy-reading language, to the honest, personal stories of adolescent parents, to the carefully selected photographs, to the loving attention given to the most sensitive issues of teen parenting, Jeanne keeps the focus on the unique needs of her youthful audience.

I was surprised when Jeanne asked me to write this foreword for her book. My first internal response was to say, "Wouldn't it be better to have a mom write this?" As I more carefully considered her invitation, I realized that her request simply reflected Jeanne's belief that dads, regardless of their age and relationship to their child's mother, are important. She sees dads as having a far more significant role than that of child support provider. For dads everywhere, of all ages, I thank her. Certainly her chapter, "For Dad Only," demonstrates her commitment to father involvement. However, the implied expectation that dads will want to be invested fathers is woven throughout her book, and this speaks most clearly of Jeanne's belief in active fathering.

In Carlisle, the little Iowa town in which I live, I've been able to experience again (but from a safer distance), the agony and the ecstasy of new parenthood — in the extreme. Carlisle's Kenny and Bobbi McCaughey, Dad and Mom of the now world-famous McCaughey septuplets, live only about four blocks from our house. Not long ago, on a beautiful early spring day, they took the seven five-month-olds and the one two-year-old out for a stroll. The two four-seat strollers looked like mini-Mack trucks as they slowly moved down the sidewalk. All in one breath I said, "Thank God, it's not me," and "Thank God, they have help with those kids." Over the past few months Carlisle has become one huge extended family for the McCaugheys. Without caring community members to provide assistance with rocking, feeding, diapering, consoling, and sleeping, Kenny and Bobbi would surely be beyond wit's end by now. Instead, they are doing well, and the children are thriving, once again reminding us of the power of extended families.

In the foreword of the first edition of this book, Martha Bullock Lamberts wrote, "Readers have access to a kind of extended family in book format — one that is knowledgeable, and warmly caring." Unlike the McCaugheys, teen parents do not always have the help of extended families. Nonetheless, to an adolescent parent, one child may seem like seven. For this reason, Jeanne Warren Lindsay's *Your Baby's First Year* is a true gift to teen moms and dads.

Tom Klaus, M.S.
Program Director, IT TAKES TWO
Young Women's Resource Center
Des Moines, Iowa

ACKNOWLEDGMENTS

I am grateful to Sally McCullough, Jean Brunelli, and Mary Grayce Zentis who made time to read and critique part or all of this revised edition, and to all those who read the earlier edition. Their comments were invaluable.

Perhaps even more important is the input from teen parents, the young people we interviewed, and whose wisdom is scattered throughout the book. For the first edition, we quoted 66 young people. For this revised edition, 54 more were interviewed, and many of this group are quoted here. They include Angelina Rojas, Danielle Alston, Jason Banks, Isabel Franco, Janelle Byers, Jill Winkler, Laura Lilio, Lisa Grimes, Maria Almarez, Melisa Romero, Robin Stanley, Satrina Broussard, Tiffany McLean, and Tiffany Torres. Others are quoted and acknowledged in the other books in the *Teens Parenting* series. We also appreciate the many other teenage parents whose insightful quotes are retained from the earlier edition.

David Crawford, teacher in the Teen Parent Program, William Daylor High School, Sacramento, supplied most of the photographs. His models were his wonderful students. Carole Blum and Jean Brunelli also provided photographs for this edition, and I appreciate each one.

Tim Rinker is the cover artist, and Steve Lindsay helped design the book. I am grateful for the contributions of all of these talented people.

Carole Blum and Karen Blake again helped with the proofreading and kept Morning Glory Press alive and well during book production time. I thank them for their valuable support.

I'm especially grateful to Bob who continues to be supportive even during those times when the current book seems all important. I think he knows he's even *more* important to me.

Jeanne Lindsay

To the young parents
who share so freely on these pages

Parenting is indeed a wonderful challenge.

Part I

Those First Months

You come home with a newborn who appears to need you constantly. Or she may sleep much of the time in the early weeks, and demand more of your attention a month or two later. Whatever her pattern, comfort is what she wants and needs.

In the following three chapters, you'll learn about parenting during these first three or four months. First, the basics —dealing with crying, bathing your baby, changing diapers, handling your own frustrations.

Food, of course, is a big issue for a tiny baby (and for all of us). The second chapter focuses on feeding your infant, whether by breastfeeding or with bottles.

How can one little person change so rapidly in just three or four months? Those amazing changes are discussed in chapter 3, along with the impact you, the parent, have on his development, physical, emotional, and intellectual.

You're starting a wonderfully challenging journey.

Your new life as a parent has begun.

1

Beginning Life
With Your Baby

The house was full of people those first two weeks, and that was the worst part of it. I wish they could have waited until a couple of weeks after he was born. I was real tired. It doesn't seem like you ever sleep like you used to.

You get home, and he's so tiny you breastfeed every two hours. I was worn out, but my mom cooked for me and kept things clean.

It's funny — nothing would ever wake me up before, but when he makes the slightest cry, I wake up. I'll be in the kitchen, the washer is going, noise everywhere, and I'll hear him.

Adriana, 16 - Danny, 3 months

A Blur of Tiredness

Those first weeks with your new baby may seem like a blur, a time of constant activity and tiredness. Your baby may need to be fed every couple of hours. She may be awake much of the night, then sleep most of the day.

Have patience with her. The first couple of weeks I was impatient because I wanted to sleep, and Jenny wouldn't sleep.

Sleep while your baby is sleeping. I had to wash clothes, hang them up, fold them, wash the dishes. You don't have time to sleep, but you have to make time. Sleep was important to me.

Rosita, 18 - Jenny, 4 weeks

When you come home from the hospital, you will probably be tired, and baby's demands won't give you much time to rest.

If you had an episiotomy (small cut made to enlarge the vaginal opening), your stitches may hurt the first few days. If you had a C-section (caesarean delivery), your recovery from childbirth will be slower.

It was hard when I first came home. I was in pain at first, and sitting was hard.

Nick really wasn't that much trouble, except the whole first month he had his days and nights all mixed up.

Theresa, 16 - Nick, 6 months

Most parents experience these feelings. Most parents also experience the joy of early parenting. Holding your tiny helpless baby is a special and usually wonderful feeling.

Chapter 12, *Your Pregnancy and Newborn Journey,* describes a newborn in detail.

"He's a real good father. He loves him very much."

Let Dad Help

If you're with your baby's father, whether or not you're married and/or living together, encourage him to be involved in baby care. When he is, everyone wins. You'll have some of the help you need with baby. The more dad does with baby, the faster he'll bond with his child. Your baby wins by having two loving parents.

> *Babies want all of your attention. Jay's father lives with us and does his fair share. He changes Jay's diapers, gives him a bath, feeds him. He's a real good father —he loves Jay very much.*
>
> Bev, 17 - Jay, 8 months

Be careful that you, the baby's mom, don't suggest through words or actions that only you know what to do when baby cries. If you criticize your husband/boyfriend, he may soon decide that caring for baby is, indeed, your job, not his to share. You'll end up getting tired and perhaps feeling upset. He may decide he's not needed, and that he's being left out of this whole parenting business.

Perhaps he hasn't had much experience with tiny infants. If he seems afraid of doing the wrong thing, show him how to diaper, feed, and rock baby. With practice, he may feel better about the whole situation.

Peaceful Home Is Needed

In addition to simple comfort, baby prefers a generally peaceful home. If her parents argue a lot, she will sense it. She may become as upset as they are.

One young mother described her first month with her baby. She lived with the baby's father, and their relationship was not going well.

The baby cried a great deal which proved to be the breaking point in his parents' relationship. Kimberly was so tired from caring for little Karl that she had no time left for Tom. She also resented the fact that he refused to help her take care of their baby. Tom, in turn, felt left out and generally unhappy. One night they had another terrible argument. Kimberly decided to take Karl and move back with her mother:

I stayed with Tom for two more days, but we weren't speaking. Karl was upset the whole time. In fact, he cried a lot from the day we came home from the hospital.

As soon as we moved in with my mother, Karl began sleeping through the night. He's been an entirely different baby. Instead of crying all the time, he's smiling at us now. I know all that arguing was hard on him. I'm glad I finally found the courage to leave.

Kimberly, 17 - Karl, 2 months

Jeanne, mother of two-month-old Eric, explained:

*Your home life has a lot to do with a child. If I'm
tense, he is, too. If a lot of yelling goes on, it bothers
the baby.*

*Sometimes Mike and I fight, but we don't in front of
the baby. It's bad to do that because he can feel the
tension, and it's not good for him. You would think a
two-month-old baby wouldn't know, but they do. If
they hear you fighting, it's bad.*

Enjoy Your Infant

*My grandmother is afraid I'll spoil her because
when Jenilee cries, I pick her up. I believe she cries
for a reason and that you can't spoil a newborn, so I
don't really pay attention to Grandma.*

*When Jenilee cries I pick her up and hold her
against my chest with her face where she can hear my
heart beat. Or I walk her while I'm standing up. She
likes me to walk around with her. Or I start talking
with her. She likes to listen to my voice.*

Lacey, 16 - Jenilee, 1 month

The most important part of caring for your baby is
getting to know her — bonding together as closely as
possible. If you interact a lot with baby, hold her, talk to
her, carry on conversations whenever she's awake, you'll
find the bonding happens just the way it should.

Your newborn's main interest is his own comfort. When
he's hungry, he wants and needs to be fed *now*. He may
hate wet or messy diapers, or he may not seem to notice. If
he doesn't like them, he lets you know by crying. Even if
you've fed and changed him, and you know he's neither
too warm nor too cold, he may still cry. Often it's because
he's lonely. Or he may be a colicky baby who just cries

more than some babies do. (See page 63.)

Your main job as a parent of a newborn infant is to help him be as comfortable as possible. You feed him when he's hungry, change his diaper when necessary, hold him when he wants you to. But most of his days and nights the typical newborn spends sleeping.

When you lay him down to sleep, always place him on his back. SIDS (Sudden Infant Death Syndrome) is much less likely to happen to babies who sleep on their backs.

When he's awake and needs you, you're the one who talks, smiles, interacts with him. At first, he may not appear to pay much attention to you, but it's important that you talk to him from the day he's born.

Your "conversations" with him help him learn to trust you and the rest of his world. When you talk with him, you're already helping him work toward developing his language skills.

Bathing Your Newborn

My mother gave Orlando his first bath. She offered for me to do it, but I let her the first two times. I was totally scared when I first bathed him. I would cry because he cried. I think he didn't like to be naked at first, but now he loves it.

Holly, 17 - Orlando, 5 months

We know baby wants to be comfortable. To be comfortable, she needs to be kept clean.

Until your baby's navel cord drops off, she shouldn't be put in water. Just give her a "sponge" bath — lay her on a towel in a warm room and wash her with a soapy washcloth. Then rinse her off thoroughly and dry her.

After the cord drops off, you can give baby a real bath. Wash his head and face first. Don't use soap on his face, but wash his hair with plain soap or baby shampoo at least once a week. After you've washed and dried his face, use your hand to lather the rest of his body with plain soap. Wash the baby's genitals just as you do the rest of his body. Rinse him thoroughly, wrap him in a towel, and pat him dry. Be sure you talk to him the entire time.

If your kitchen sink is big enough, you might prefer to bathe your baby there. It's a comfortable height, and you don't have to lift the tub to empty the water. You have to be extra careful not to let baby slip and get hurt on the faucets.

If you live in a family home with a lot of different people, however, using the sink may interfere with their routine. If you do wash baby in the sink, clean it thoroughly before and after her bath.

Always test the water to be sure it isn't too hot. Stick your elbow in it. It's more sensitive to temperature than your hands are.

Never leave baby alone in her bath.

> *First bath? He didn't like it. He screamed and cried and it scared me. I still haven't found a good technique because he doesn't like to take baths.*
>
> *For the first month and a half I just gave him a sponge bath like I did when he was first born. He doesn't mind that. My mom and my grandmother think it's kind of silly. They thought I should just give him a bath, but I feel whatever works for me and him is the best thing so . . . the sponge bath worked well.*
>
> Brooke, 18 - Blair, 3 months

Even though some infants find bathtime relaxing and soothing, a lot of tiny babies don't like their bath. Sometimes when you put her in the water, she may shiver. If she does, shorten her bath, then wrap her in a towel. And there's nothing wrong with bathing a baby by using a washcloth to wash her while she lies on the towel, as

Brooke did. And babies don't *have* to have a bath every day.

Of course you'll clean her bottom thoroughly when you change her. A daily bath is a nice part of her routine — if she's okay about it. If she hates it, bathe her every other day, perhaps only a sponge bath for a little longer.

One mother referred to the first bath as "trying to hold on to a wet seal." She continued:

A lot of girls are scared to hold the baby because he's too slippery. He's little, but he's a person, too, and you shouldn't be afraid of holding him.

Gary likes his bath now, and he laughs a little when I wash his hair with warm water. He cries when I take him out because he's cold.

                                              Leica, 18 - Gary, 3 months

Don't try to clean any body opening (nose, ears, navel) with cotton-tipped sticks. Anything you can't clean with a corner of a washcloth doesn't need cleaning. You don't need to use cream, lotion, or powder on baby's body either. In fact, some of these products may irritate her skin. Clean babies smell good without the help of these items.

Don't worry when your baby touches his/her genitals. S/he's curious about this part of his/her body. Touching the genitals is as normal and certainly as harmless as touching one's nose.

The Diaper Question

I was using a big name brand of diapers, but now I'm going to the cheapest kind. I decided on dispos-able diapers out of laziness and because of the smell of having the diapers in the house. And I didn't want the mess of cleaning them out in the toilet.

                                                                    Bev

Keeping her clean and dry is important for her comfort.

Disposable diapers seem to be used "by everyone." They're easy to use, and often are considered simply another necessary expense of baby care. It's still possible, however, to buy cloth diapers and wash them yourself. You'd spend less money. Cloth diapers are also kinder to our environment.

> *I use cloth diapers because of the money. Every week I had to buy a bag of diapers —nearly $100 a month! For 88 diapers it's over $20. I started using cloth when he was two or three months old.*
>
> *I think a lot of girls use the disposables because they're lazy. They think changing cloth diapers is gross. Sometimes they're afraid they'll stick the baby with the pins. I use the cloth kind with the velcro.*
>
> Delia, 15 - Kelsey, 7 months

Before you decide whether to use a diaper service, disposables, or diapers you wash yourself, figure out the comparative cost in your area.

It is indeed easier to use either disposable diapers or diapers from a commercial service. If you have plenty of money, take your pick. In any case, you'll probably want one or two disposables and throw-away wipes in the diaper bag for convenience. Most of us would find several hundred extra dollars quite welcome at the end of the year. That's the difference in cost between using disposable diapers or the wash-your-own kind. If you have good laundry facilities, washing diapers isn't hard. And you can always fold them while you watch television.

I use cloth diapers. I don't like disposables. Robin gets rashes from paper and not from cloth diapers. If you rinse them out, they don't stink. I put them in the washer before school, and put them in the dryer when I get home. I fold them after she goes to sleep.

Melinda, 15 - Robin, 9 months

Why Do Babies Cry?

The first few months I was having a heart attack because it was all new to me. I'd say, "What's wrong with him? I gave him his bottle. I changed him."

Then I would start crying. I would call my mom or my mother-in-law. I'd get real nervous, but after the first three months, we kind of got the hang of it.

Ernesta 20 - Jeremy, 3; Osvaldo, 5 months

Babies cry for many reasons other than colic. Most often, she's simply hungry. The solution is also simple. Feed her.

If she cries after being fed, is it possible she still needs burping? Most babies can burp when you rub or pat their backs gently for a minute or two. Others need to have their backs patted or rubbed for a longer time.

Some babies cry because of a wet or messy diaper. Again, the solution is simple. Change her.

Other babies can't seem to fall asleep without fussing a lot. If you're sure your baby isn't hungry, too cold or too warm, and doesn't need her diaper changed, and she still cries, she may need to be held for awhile.

Don't worry about spoiling her. Being there when she needs you helps her learn to trust her world. If she trusts her needs will be met, she's likely to cry less in the future.

Important Note

Sometimes you'll do everything you can to help your baby be comfortable, and she'll still cry. Always remember she is *not* crying to upset you. She isn't crying because you've spoiled her. She's crying because it's the only way she can tell you that she needs you.

Sometimes taking her outside will help. She may stop crying if she has something new and different to watch. A ride in the car (safely secured in her carseat) may calm her.

Babies cry for many reasons. Most often, he's simply hungry.

Some mothers report their babies fall asleep almost the instant the car starts.

Some babies go to sleep most easily when they're in their swing. Soft music might help. A little music box beside their bed soothes some babies.

You May Get Frustrated

Jesse was very fussy today. God, sometimes I wish I could just get up and leave because I'm so tired of not being able to do whatever I want. I'm trying not to have these feelings, but I can't help it. I just wonder, are they wrong? Am I a horrible mother for thinking like that? I hope not.

Frederica, 16 - Jesse, 5 months

Of course Frederica is not a bad mother for having these very real feelings. Most of us get more tense as the baby cries harder.

The problem then is that the baby feels the parent's tenseness and is even more upset.

Acting on one's frustration by hurting the baby is certainly wrong. Some parents resort to child abuse. Perhaps you've heard an older parent angrily say to a crying child, "If you don't quit that crying, you're getting a spanking." That's not very sensible, is it? It doesn't help the parent, and it certainly doesn't make the child feel better.

Sometimes a parent may feel like shaking the baby. Shaking is absolutely the wrong thing to do. Shaking can damage a baby's brain. See that no one *ever* shakes your baby.

When you're upset because of baby's crying, you'll help your baby if you can possibly relax. Try thinking about something you really like doing or fantasizing about your favorite place. Your baby may relax as you do.

Sometimes your baby will cry because she doesn't feel

well. Is she feverish? Is she teething? See chapter 4 for more about caring for baby when she's not feeling well.

If your bottle-fed baby cries a lot, perhaps her formula isn't right for her. Talk with your health professional. Perhaps she will suggest a different formula.

As you get to know your baby, you'll find still other ways to help her be more comfortable.

My frustrations? I just deal with it. I don't get angry at Jenilee. Sometimes I get upset because I'm real tired and I'm trying to sleep and she doesn't want to sleep. I get up and play with her and talk with her. I think about my baby first.

Lacey

She's Changing Rapidly

Racquelle is seven weeks old now. She looks more like a little girl, and she's a lot bigger than when she was born. At first I was holding her constantly. Now I lay a blanket down, and she's content to lie there.

Cheryl, 15 - Racquelle, 2 months

As you care for your baby, you'll see tremendous changes during her first weeks "on the outside." You're working hard and you may be exhausted, but watching her develop makes it all worthwhile.

Be sure you talk to your baby from the minute she's born. As each week passes, she will respond more and more to your conversation. You, her parent, are the most important person in her world. Enjoy!

As we've stressed before, feed him when he's hungry. Change him when he's wet. Talk to him and hold him when he's lonely. He'll reward you by responding to you more and more as the days go by.

Your journey through parenthood has begun.

Breastfeeding is good for both babies and moms.

2

Food —
Along with Love

Paula only cries when she's hungry, cold or lonely. Last night she was waking up every 15 minutes. She wanted me to hold her until she went to sleep.

Breastfeeding is working fine. I didn't have much soreness, only the second day when my milk came in. I gave her a little water once, but she doesn't seem to need that since she's breastfeeding.

Deanna, 15 - Paula, 3 weeks

Patty cries about the average. I don't always feed her because I can tell if she's hungry. I just pat her on her back and she goes back to sleep. She likes a pacifier, too.

*Sometimes she sleeps four or five hours. I'll feed
her at 10 p.m., and she won't wake up until 3 or 4
a.m. During the day she goes three to four hours
without eating.*

*I don't let her cry for long. My mom says I should
so she can exercise her lungs, but I don't agree.*

Beth, 18 - Patty, 3 weeks

Let Baby Set Mealtime

How often should you feed baby? Years ago, some
"experts" recommended feeding her by the clock. She
should eat every four hours, according to this theory.
Occasionally an extra small baby might need to be fed
every three hours. We now think this was a terrible theory.
Tiny babies need to be fed when they're hungry. They can't
tell time for a few years yet, so their hunger pains are *not*
clock directed. They're simply hungry when they're hungry. And they *don't* cry to exercise their lungs!

During the first couple of months most of your baby's
crying is probably due to hunger. Offer her your breast or a
bottle first. If she doesn't want food, naturally you don't try
to force her to eat. You look for other reasons for her
crying, like wet or dirty diapers. But first you offer breast
or formula.

Starting with Breastfeeding

*Why did I breastfeed? Because I feel it's healthier
for the baby and it's easier instead of making a bottle.
David* (teacher) *always tells us it's more nutritious, it
helps you have a bond with your baby. Anybody could
feed your baby with a bottle.*

Lacey, 16 - Jenilee, 1 month

Breastfeeding is generally the ideal food for baby. It's
also good for mom — no bottles to clean, no formula to

mix, and it's always the right temperature.

Chapter 11, *Your Pregnancy and Newborn Journey,* includes lots of information about breastfeeding — why, how, when, and where. We'll briefly repeat the high points.

First, why breastfeed? It's better for your baby, and can be extremely satisfying for mom. It's cheaper, and it's more convenient.

Even if you breastfeed your baby for only a few days, you'll be giving him extra protection against illness. Your breasts don't produce milk for two or three days after delivery. Instead, they produce colostrum, a yellowish substance which will help your baby fight off colds and other illnesses. Those first few days of breastfeeding give your baby a good start in life.

So how do you start? To nurse your baby, hold him on his side facing you, tummy to tummy. Touch his lower lip, and he'll open his mouth. When his mouth opens wide, bring him to your nipple.

You probably will have a little soreness that first week. Letting your nipples air dry after feeding will help. So will rubbing a little breast milk into the sore area after each feeding. Changing positions with each feeding will also minimize soreness.

Latching on is the term we use for the baby getting your nipple into his mouth. The important thing is to get as much as possible of the areola (dark area around the nipple) into his mouth as he sucks. If he latches on properly, your nipples shouldn't get sore. If it hurts, break the suction and take him off, then latch him on with more of the areola in his mouth.

The more your baby sucks, the more milk your body will produce. To give breastfeeding a good start, it's best not to give baby a bottle during the first month.

If your baby seems hungrier after the first couple of

weeks, she probably is. She's reached a growth spurt where she needs more milk. If you're breastfeeding, her increased hunger doesn't mean you reach for the formula. Instead, you nurse her more often. Within a day or two your breasts will "catch up" with her hunger.

You may find this happening again when she's about six weeks old, and again at three months. As long as you nurse her more often, your breasts will work the magic of producing more milk as she needs it.

It's not necessary to hide in your bedroom while you breastfeed. Babies like to eat when they get hungry, just as we do, only it's much harder for them to wait awhile. You should be able to breastfeed almost anywhere by throwing a blanket over your baby.

One time we were at Mike's baseball game, and I went to the car to feed Eric. When Mike and his friends came back, I had him all covered up with a blanket while I nursed him. They said, "Sh-h, he's asleep." I smiled and nodded.

Jeanne, 16 - Eric, 2 months

Taking Care of You

I'm breastfeeding Jenny. Once in awhile I give her a bottle. I figure God intended me to breastfeed, that it's the right kind of milk for my baby. And I haven't had any problems with breastfeeding.

It seems like I'm closer to her when I breastfeed her because she looks at me, and sometimes she smiles. And in the night I don't have to warm any bottle, just breastfeed her.

Rosita, 18 - Jenny, 4 weeks

When you're caring for a baby, you especially need to take good care of yourself. While you're breastfeeding, it's extra important that you eat the nutritious foods you needed while you were pregnant. You need about 500 extra calories each day. A sandwich and two extra glasses of milk in addition to your "regular" nutritious diet should be enough.

Drink enough liquids, too. You need 12 to 16 glasses daily of water, milk, fruit juices, etc. "Liquids" is the key word. You don't have to drink milk to make breastmilk. If you like it or can drink it, include it as part of your liquids. If not, get your calcium from other sources such as green leafy vegetables and calcium-fortified orange juice.

It's best for the baby if you can limit your drinking of coffee, tea, and soft drinks to two cups each day. Avoid caffeinated beverages. Choose decaf versions instead.

When you nurse your baby, sit (or lie) in a comfortable place. Put your feet up and enjoy your baby. Drink one of those many glasses of liquid you need each day. Learn to relax while you're feeding baby. Your milk comes in more easily if you're relaxed. Baby will be pleased!

It's absolutely necessary that you get enough rest if you're taking care of a little baby. If you get too tired, you may not be able to produce as much milk. Even if you're bottle-feeding, your baby doesn't need an exhausted mother. *Take care of yourself.*

Your healthcare provider will want to see you four to six weeks after your baby is born. Be *sure* to keep this appointment. She will check your health and make sure you're recovering well from pregnancy and delivery. If you haven't already talked with her about birth control, this is a good time to do so.

Breastfeeding for a Little While

You may choose to breastfeed a few days because you know how good colostrum is for your baby, then switch to bottles. Or you may decide not to breastfeed at all.

Adriana and Shauntika each breastfed for awhile, then decided to switch to bottles:

I was breastfeeding during the weeks I was out of school. It was great but I stopped when I went back to school.

At first it was hard because I didn't know what I was doing. My breasts hurt after I stopped. I stopped breastfeeding on Saturday and he started on the bottle on Sunday.

Shauntika, 17 - Dante, 5 months

I stopped slowly. I'd breastfeed her when she woke up at 5 a.m. because that was more convenient. I didn't have to get up and make a bottle. At first, I'd give her a bottle at school, then breastfeed her at home. Then I had less milk, and it all worked out.

Adriana, 18 - Rachel, 3 months

Adriana was wise to stop breastfeeding gradually. Deciding to switch baby from breast to bottle suddenly is hard on baby and hard on mom. No wonder Shauntika's breasts hurt. If you simply quit breastfeeding one day, your body will continue producing milk for awhile. Your breasts will hurt and you might develop a breast infection.

It's far better to give her a bottle for one of her feedings each day for a few days, then cut out another breastfeeding, then another, until you're feeding her from the bottle all the time. You will both adjust to the change much better than if you switch suddenly.

Some Choose Bottle-Feeding

Bottle-feeding just seemed normal to me. I was smoking a lot, and they told me I shouldn't breastfeed because I'd give Mona the nicotine.

Ellie, 17 - Mona, 11 months

In a few situations formula is actually better for baby. If a mother must take medicine which would harm her baby, she shouldn't breastfeed. If she is on drugs or if she smokes a lot, feeding her baby formula would be wiser than breastfeeding. (Staying away from drugs and cigarettes is, of course, the most caring approach.)

If you decide to bottle-feed, you can choose from ready-to-use, concentrated, or powdered formula. The ready-to-use formula is the most expensive and the easiest to use. Whichever formula you choose, follow instructions carefully. Be sure bottles and nipples are absolutely clean. Boil the water and let it cool before you mix it with either the concentrated or powdered formula. Always check the temperature of the formula before giving it to baby.

Some babies are allergic to cow's milk. Ask your healthcare provider if your baby seems to have problems. She will probably prescribe a formula made of soybean powder.

Heating baby's bottle in the microwave oven is a dangerous practice. While the bottle may feel cool, the formula inside could be hot enough to burn your baby.

Baby Needs Burping

Usually I feed him six ounces, and I burp him every two ounces. I place the burp rag over my left shoulder. I pat his back and rub him in a forward stroke. If he gets to where he's real colicky and cranky, I put him on his stomach and burp him that way.

Chelsea, 19 - Clancy, 2 months

Whether you breast- or bottle-feed, hold your baby close while you feed her. This is a wonderful getting-acquainted time for both of you. As you talk and smile with her, you'll feel even closer to each other.

Some babies need burping several times during a feeding

while others don't want or need their meal interrupted.
You'll be sensitive to *your* baby's needs. Several burping
positions work:

• Hold her upright against your shoulder.

• Support her in a sitting position on your lap.

• Lay her on her stomach across your knees.

Whichever position you choose, rub or pat her back
gently until she burps. For many babies, this happens fairly
quickly, while others need several minutes of help with the
important job of burping:

> *Keonia often has too much gas in her stomach.*
> *When that happens, I spend ten to twenty minutes*
> *burping her. If I don't, she'll spit up again.*
>
> Lei, 16 - Keonia, 4 months

Is She Getting Enough?

> *I pretty much fed him on demand every 31/2 to four*
> *hours. He was a good baby. He'd get up to eat at*
> *night, then go right back to sleep.*
>
> *My cousin doesn't believe in feeding on demand.*
> *She says Orlando will get fat, that he'll be obsessed*
> *with food when he gets older. But Orlando knows*
> *when to eat.*
>
> Holly, 17 - Orlando, 5 months

How do you know if your baby is getting enough milk?
If you bottle-feed, your doctor will tell you about how
much formula your baby needs. At times, baby won't finish
her bottle. You don't need to worry. She probably wasn't as
hungry as usual. Her appetite will vary from feeding to
feeding. "Enough" at one meal may not be enough next
time. You will find she eats about the same *total* amount of
formula each day.

If you're breastfeeding, your baby will "tell" you if

she's getting enough milk. She's getting plenty if:

- She has at least six to eight wet diapers each day after one week of age.
- She seems satisfied for at least one or two hours after each feeding.
- She seems to be gaining weight and is active when she's awake.

Especially if you're breastfeeding, your baby doesn't need water the first four to six months.

If he has a fever or diarrhea, however, he needs extra water. If baby has the hiccups, offer him a sip of water from a teaspoon. By the time he's four months old, you can try giving baby a little water from a small cup. He may be ready to take a couple of tiny sips.

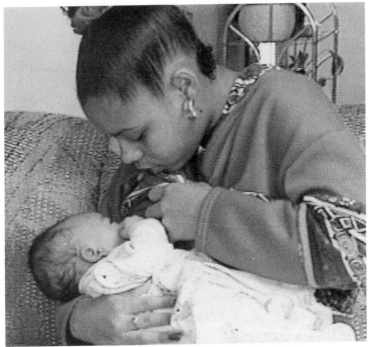

"I feel closer to her when I'm breastfeeding."

No Propped Bottles — Ever

*I don't like bottle propping. Babies choke. They
drink it too fast and they can't swallow it.*

Chelsea, 19 - Clancy, 2 months

Whenever you give your baby a bottle, *always* be sure
you hold him. Don't ever lay him down and prop his bottle
in his mouth, then leave him to drink alone.

First of all, he needs the love and emotional support he'll
feel from being in your arms. He also needs eye contact
with you while he's eating. These happenings are all
extremely important to baby.

*I blew it with my mother-in-law yesterday. She's
been wanting to keep little Eric for a few hours, and I
finally took him over there. I thought he'd be all right
while I did some shopping. I came back about two
hours later, and I couldn't believe my eyes.*

*My mother-in-law was working in the kitchen, and
there Eric was on the couch — with a bottle propped
in his mouth! You should have seen him. His little
hands were all clenched, and his whole body looked
tense and uptight. Usually when he's eating, he waves
his arms and has such a good time.*

*I was furious. I took a deep breath and said, "If
you don't have time to hold him while he eats, I do."
I picked him up and went home!*

*Babies need to be held while they're eating. They
need that love and attention. Besides, bottle-propping
is dangerous — he could choke, and it could cause an
ear infection. If she ever keeps him again, she'd better
not prop his bottle!*

Jeanne

As Jeanne said, in addition to the loving he gets from
being held while he eats, he's also less likely to have an ear

infection if you don't ever prop his bottle. Many ear infections are caused by baby drinking from a propped bottle. The passageway from the ear to the throat doesn't drain well in infancy. Formula, if not "served" properly, can go back to his ears and cause an infection.

If you need another reason for holding baby while you feed him, remember that a baby with a propped bottle can spit up and choke on the milk curd. He's unable to spit it out if a bottle is propped in his mouth.

He May Need a Pacifier

He's very content. He can't live without his pacifier. He will usually take one at night when he's going to bed. It's like his security blanket. I lay him down and rub it against his lips, and he takes it.

Chelsea

Babies need a lot of sucking. Breastfed babies can usually suck more while eating than bottle-fed babies. If the formula in the bottle is gone, it's gone, while the breast keeps producing a dribble of milk. A baby who needs lots of sucking can get it there.

In fact, some experts agree breastfeeding will work better if you *don't* give baby a pacifier for the first month or so.

Lots of babies, however, whether breastfed or bottle-fed, need still more sucking. Your baby may find her fist soon after birth. (Many babies suck their thumbs while still in mother's womb.)

If she seems to want more sucking, offer her a pacifier. If you're breastfeeding, offer it only after nursing her and she still seems to want to suck. That way, you're not accidentally putting off a feeding.

Even if the neighbors frown, giving your baby a pacifier

is fine. Throw it away as soon as she doesn't seem to need the extra sucking, probably before the end of the first year.

Just don't substitute the pacifier for the attention, food, or diaper change she wants and needs when she's crying.

No Solid Food Yet

Babies under four to six months of age don't need and shouldn't have anything to eat except breast milk or formula. Their digestive systems aren't ready for other foods.

Feeding a two-month-old baby cereal in the evening is not going to help him sleep all night. It may make him cross and fussy the next day because of problems with digestion caused by the cereal. If so, he may be so tired by night that he'll sleep better. But don't give the cereal credit for the sleep.

Vitamin/Mineral Supplements

If you're breastfeeding your baby, continue taking your prenatal vitamins for two or three months after delivery. If you do, your baby won't need an extra vitamin supplement. She gets her vitamins through your milk, and an extra dose wouldn't be good for her.

Vitamins. Commercially prepared formula contains enough vitamin D for baby.

Fluoride. Whether you're breastfeeding or bottle-feeding, your baby needs fluoride. In some areas this is in the water supply. Ask your healthcare provider about it. If it's not already in your water supply, the doctor may prescribe a fluoride supplement beginning in the early months. Give exactly as prescribed. Don't overdose!

Getting enough fluoride helps prevent cavities in our teeth while too much fluoride can be a problem. It can lead to discolored teeth. Since the amount of fluoride in your water supply may be high or low, it's important that you ask your healthcare provider how much, if any, fluoride supplement your baby needs.

Iron. If you're eating enough nutritious, iron-rich foods, your breast milk will provide enough iron for your baby for about four months. At that time, your healthcare provider may suggest an iron supplement. Or she may tell you it's all right to start feeding baby an iron-fortified cereal.

Most commercial formulas contain iron. Your doctor will help you decide which one is best for your baby.

Call WIC for Food Expense Help

If it's hard for you to get enough of the right foods for yourself while you're breastfeeding, call your Public Health Department for information about WIC (Special Supplemental Feeding Program for Women, Infants, and Children). You may be able to get coupons for certain foods you need. In many communities, the fact that you're a teenage mother may make you eligible for help from WIC.

WIC also provides help in buying nutritious foods for pregnant women and for baby's formula.

The food stamp program helps extend food dollars for eligible families. Ask your social worker for information.

Your Journey Together

Feeding your baby, whether by breast or bottle, is an important part of keeping her comfortable. Each mealtime is a special time of closeness, warmth, and love as you talk and gaze into each other's eyes.

Both you and your baby are off to a good start on your journey together.

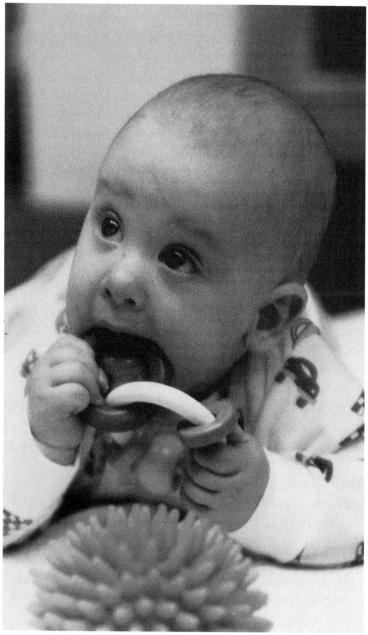

Putting things in his mouth is his way of finding out more about them.

3

His World Changes

Juan tries to talk back to me, and he makes noises. He's usually happy and has a big smile. He laughs out loud.

He sleeps through the night. When he woke up in the morning, he used to cry right away. Now he plays awhile until I wake up. He sleeps with a bear, and when he wakes up, he talks to it. He goes all over the place on his bed, turning back and forth.

Picking him up before, he was just there, but now he has a lot of personality. He loves his bath — even likes his hair washed. It makes him tired, ready to sleep.

Ginny, 17 - Juan, 4 months

How Is He Changing?

Right now Clancy is real alert. He's awake a lot which I like because it gives me an opportunity to bond with him. I feel like I can't really bond with him when he's sleepy. I play with him, and I read books to him. Usually he will fall asleep when I read to him. It gives me a real good feeling.

Chelsea, 19 - Clancy, 2 months

By the time he's two months old, baby's world *and yours* is changing rapidly. By the time he's four months old, that usually sleepy infant turns into a little person who can "do something."

As a starter, your baby's control of his head will change rapidly. At birth, he has little control over that heavy head. He needs you to support his head when you lift and hold him. A month later, he still needs his head supported. If you put him on his tummy, however, he can now lift his head a little and turn it from side to side. By two months, he can lift it up and keep it up for a few seconds.

When he's three months old, his neck and upper back muscles have grown stronger. On his tummy, he can prop himself on his arms and hold his head up. If you pick him up when he's lying on his back, his head should no longer fall backward as you lift him. Compared to his skills in this area at birth, he has improved remarkably.

He's Smiling Now

What's he like at three months? Oh, he's so alert. He has big bright eyes. His eyes are deep. He loves to be talked to. He wants you to talk to him always. He will turn his head. Ever since he was born he has responded to noises. He smiles, he coos. I have never seen a baby like him. He's a happy baby.

Brooke, 18 - Blair, 3 months

Perhaps the most exciting thing a two-month-old does is smile. If she feels good, she'll smile at almost anyone.

Four months is an especially popular age for taking pictures for sending to grandparents. You can almost depend on baby to smile and look great while you're clicking the camera. By this time, too, she will probably be giggling and laughing out loud.

About a week ago Gary discovered his feet. He pulls on them, tries to stick them in his mouth. He coos, yells, screams all the time.

He's starting to laugh out loud now. He's happy all the time except when he's wet or hungry.

Leica, 18 - Gary, 3 months

You may stay home with your baby during the first month or six weeks. Soon, however, she will like going outside for a walk or to the park:

For the past couple of days we've been going to the Regional Park, all of us —father-in-law, mother-in-law, sisters-in-law, baby, husband, and I. It was so hot at home that we couldn't stand it.

Barbi enjoyed it. She was in her stroller, and I took her for a long stroll around the park. She liked that. She looked at all the trees, and we had fun. We stopped at the playground so my sisters-in-law could play. I fed Barbi, and she went to sleep. We stayed at the park for nearly two hours.

Sandi, 16 - Barbi, 2 months

He Loves Being Close to You

One thing that really bothers me is when people take their baby around in the carrier. Why can't they hold them? It's so important that babies be held when they're littler. I can see if they're sleeping, but if the

baby is wide awake, they put them in it, and set it in
front of the TV. That doesn't make sense.

Aimee, 17 - Amelia, 10 months

A baby carrier is convenient during this stage. If you're
not holding baby, and she's not sleeping in her crib, it
allows her to see more than when she's lying flat. But it's
not a substitute for arms.

Your baby is likely to prefer being in a sturdy sling
carrier on your chest over something you hold at arm's
length away from you. Wouldn't you? She can be close to
you even when you're using your hands for other activities.

When your baby is riding in the car, of course, she *must*
be in a sturdy carseat in the back facing the rear of the car.
Being in your arms while she's riding is *not* safe for her.

Hands Are Big Discovery

By three or four months, a big and important change
occurs when your baby starts looking at her hands. Sometimes this is called "hand regard."

The first month or so, her hands are fisted, and she
doesn't seem to be aware of them. She puts her fist in her
mouth and sucks on it soon after birth, but this is more a
reflex action, not a learned activity. If you put your finger
in her fist, you will be amazed at the strength of her grip,
but again, this is a reflex action.

By two months, she will follow moving objects with her
eyes. Her hand will open and close as she uses her whole
arm to reach for an object. Put a toy in her hand so she can
feel it and watch it as she moves her arm.

Within another month, she may hold one hand in front of
her face and stare at it, sometimes for several minutes.

Carol sticks her hands in her mouth, looks at them,
clasps them on her stomach. Yesterday she looked

down and got almost bug-eyed staring at her hand.

Kristyn, 17 - Carol, 3 months

She looks at her hands now partly because she can see them more clearly. During her first month or two of life, she couldn't see small nearby objects very well. The world was a little hazy for her. By the time she's three or four months old, she probably sees about as well as any adult.

As her hands become less and less fisted, she will be able to move her fingers. This gives her something more to study. You may see her staring at her hands, moving her fingers back and forth, for five to ten minutes at a time.

A week or two after baby starts staring at her hands, she may begin to bat at objects. Hold a rattle five or six inches from her eyes. She will probably not only look at it, but she may also raise her fist and try to hit it.

Lots of Changes

Carol scoots. Sometimes I put her down on one side of the blanket. When I go put clothes in the dryer, she's off the blanket when I come back.

She rolls over both from back to stomach and the other way. We help her with pillows. She can sit up for a second, then she falls back down.

Kristyn

This stage is the last time your baby will spend most of his time on his back or on his stomach. He will soon learn to turn over from back to stomach and from stomach to back. He's probably awake about half the time now, and he may seem happy much of the time. Illness, indigestion, and cutting teeth, of course, can cause unhappiness. Generally, however, things look good to a two- to four-month-old individual.

By three or four months, baby can sit up with support.

Sitting upright gives her a much better view of her world.
Think about it. How much could you see if you were
usually lying down? What a difference it makes to be able
to sit up!

*I prop Blair up in the corner of the couch and put
pillows around him. He likes that position. He can see
more. He's curious.*

Brooke

Playing with Baby

*What is Caelin like now? She smiles more. She
recognizes me when I leave the room. Before, she
would cry when I left the room but now she doesn't.
She sort of giggles. She moves her hands, and everything I give her she puts in her mouth.*

*I put a stuffed animal on top of Caelin, and she
moves it away. She watches her mobile and she
laughs. She has a little mirror, too, and she laughs at
it. And she has this cookie monster. When you hit it, it
shakes. So she kicks it because I think she likes the
vibrating.*

*When I read to Caelin, she smiles and looks at
everything on each page.*

Alaina, 17 - Caelin, 4 months

If the weather is pleasant, baby will love going outdoors.
Lay her on a blanket under a tree where she can watch the
sunlight coming through and hear the rustling of the leaves.
Don't leave her outside alone, however, unless you're
working by a window very close to her.

Babies like excitement, their version of excitement.
Instead of going to sleep right after eating, he now wants to
play. Play at this stage includes rocking and talking
together. Playing with him doesn't mean you get nothing

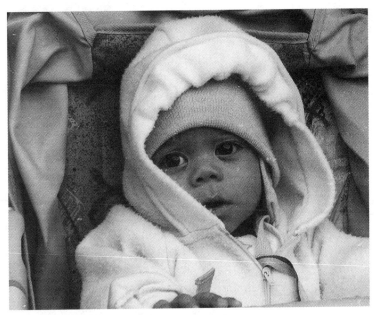

She likes to be outdoors.

else done all day. To baby, talking and singing to him while you work and he watches you is play.

The most important thing is your interaction with him. It doesn't mean complicated, time-consuming games. Baby wouldn't like that yet. It does mean giving him your full attention part of the time.

Perhaps you'll gently tickle him, move his legs slowly up and down, or give him a variety of objects to hit and grab. He'll appreciate the attention.

He's acting like a normal baby. Curious, wants to know things. He's testing out his sound effects. "I can make this noise and I can make that noise. I can hit this and make it go flying."

He hits things, makes noises, plays with his toys, puts everything in his mouth. He's real energetic.

Joel, 19 - Blair, 3 months

Choosing Toys

Her first toys need to be big enough for her to hold easily, yet too big to put in her mouth. Her toys should be washable with no sharp edges or corners. Remove any parts that come off easily. Take out the button eyes on her stuffed animals. You can embroider charming eyes for the toys, eyes that she can't choke on or swallow.

If you've been around babies, you know how different each one is from the others. They develop at different rates in different ways. Some are very active, some are quiet.

Too often parents and other people think the quiet baby is the "good" baby. In fact, the quiet baby may need more from you than does the very active baby. She needs more stimulation to help her learn about her world because she's not likely to do as much active exploring on her own.

Helping Her Exercise

I put her up on the couch and prop her so she won't fall. I exercise her. When I put her on her stomach she rolls over, first her head and then her body. And when I have her on my lap, I stand her up and she pushes down with her feet.

Alaina

We all need to exercise, even your baby. Give her plenty of opportunity to kick her feet and wave her arms freely. When she's three or four months old, she'll be able to hold her legs up. If the room is warm enough, she'll especially enjoy exercising without any clothes on.

When she's on her back, she'll soon start kicking. If she feels pressure against the soles of her feet, she may push against this pressure over and over.

You can provide pressure to her feet in two ways. First, if the end of the crib is solid, place her so she can push

against it with her feet. Second, you can briefly stand her
on a hard surface. She may enjoy pushing down with her
feet for a minute or two.

She would enjoy your help as she exercises. Hold her
feet gently and push her knees up to her stomach a few
times. *Be gentle.*

Hold her hands, or let her grasp your finger. If she's able
to hold her head up, pull her gently to a sitting position. If
her head is still wobbly, wait awhile for this one.

Help her roll from side to side on the bed. Gently
massage her legs, arms, and body. She'll love it.

Playing Means Learning

*The time they learn the most is from birth to three
years because their brains are developing so fast. It's
amazing what kids can know at the age of one if you
teach them.*

*I will talk to him like I talk to you. I understand he
will pick it up more than if I would baby talk. That's
why I'm reading to him, and do rhythmic things with
him, doing them over and over, because that's how
they learn, and I want him to be smart.*

Chelsea

Help your child do a lot of looking, feeling, and handling
of objects. Perhaps more important, give him plenty of
chances to socialize with you and other people.

Talk with him *a lot.* He will learn more easily later than
will the child who spends these early months lying in a crib
or sitting in an infant seat not doing much of anything. So
keep talking!

*I think some babies get so bored. You see them and
they look like they're spaced out. I think they need to
be stimulated.*

Play with them, talk with them, show them things, give them a lot of attention, and they will grow. I think they get real bored when they lie on their bed and look at the ceiling. Encourage them when they make noises by talking back to them. Find out what they like to do.

Ricky likes to be bounced on the bed. He likes his little legs moved, and he giggles. Then he gets so excited, and he'll tell me about it. Or he will get into his moods where he coos for an hour, and the whole family sits around and admires him.

Courtney, 15 - Ricky, 3 months

If you haven't already started reading to your baby (perhaps before she was born?), it's time. "Reading" at this stage means looking at pictures together, or perhaps baby will simply like the sound of your voice. Singing to him, of course, will please him, too.

Reading? Oh, yes. I hold Blair in my lap and read the book. Sometimes he will coo. Sometimes he sits there and pays attention like he really knows, like a big kid.

Blair likes music. If he hears me singing, he kind of hums. I sing to him a lot. I do Itsy Bitsy Spider and he gets all excited. Whenever there's music I will bounce him. He likes to bounce, and he will smile and laugh. I take off his socks and I kiss his feet. He loves it.

Brooke

Other Caregivers

Some parents stay home most of the time with their newborn baby. Especially if she's breastfeeding, mother may find it easier as well as more pleasant for both herself and the baby if she doesn't try to take him out much or attempt to leave without him during those first weeks.

By two months, however, you'll want to go out, do things on your own occasionally. Unless you have a live-in sitter, you'll need to let your sitter know where baby's things are kept and the style of care baby needs. Does he expect rocking after feeding? Is he hard to burp? Does he whimper a few minutes before falling asleep?

In addition, be sure to leave phone numbers for your doctor, a caring neighbor, the fire department, and the police department. Put the numbers where the sitter can find them easily. Always let him/her know exactly how to reach you while you're gone. Some parents leave Medicaid stickers with a sitter if they're going to be gone long.

Whenever you leave your child with someone else, it's wise to give that person a signed medical emergency card. You could state, "_____ *has my permission to obtain emergency medical care as needed for my child.*" Be sure you sign the card. Generally, medical care may not be given to a child without his/her parent's permission.

What About Family Planning?

Another baby? Not very soon. We want to wait three or four years. We're pretty careful with contraception because we don't want another baby right away. That would be hard because we'd be spending twice as much on diapers and everything else. It would make everything harder. It'll also be easier when Keegan is 3 or 4 years old because he'll know more. He won't cry as much. We've agreed to wait.
                              Randy, 17 - Keegan, 2 months

Couples need to think and talk about future family plans. How soon do you want another child? Many young mothers, married as well as single, don't want another baby right away. From a physical standpoint, their bodies need time to recuperate from the last pregnancy.

Breastfeeding won't keep you from getting pregnant. You conceive *before* a menstrual period. Even if you haven't had a period since you delivered, you can get pregnant.

See chapter 15 for more comments from young parents on this issue. Also see chapter 14, *Your Pregnancy and Newborn Journey,* for more information on family planning methods.

Babies often come by accident. If you don't want to get pregnant again soon, you and your partner need to discuss your prevention plan. You either need to abstain totally from sexual intercourse or you need to use contraception *every time.*

No Longer a Newborn

Your newborn changes more rapidly during these first four months than he ever will again. These first months offer a real challenge to baby's parents. Your major task is simply to meet his needs as much as possible.

Love him, keep him comfortable, play with him, talk to him *often*, and enjoy him.

Part II

Health Care and Family

Your baby's health depends greatly on you, his parent. You're responsible for making and keeping appointments for well-baby check-ups, and for scheduling his immunizations. It's you who will care for him when he's ill, and call his healthcare provider when necessary.

In the next chapter you will find tips for keeping your baby healthy, and for caring for him when he's ill.

Families are important to babies. Is Dad involved? Chapter 5 is written especially to him. Or are you, the mom, parenting alone? Perhaps you'll find guidance in chapter 6.

Most of us also have extended family. Especially if you're living with your parents or your partner's parents, you'll be interested in chapter 7, "Three-Generation Living."

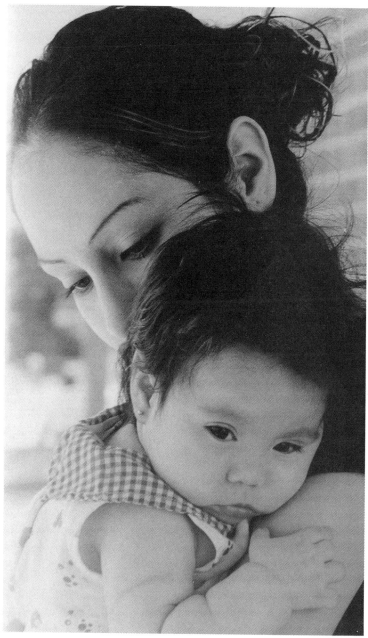

Mommy's arms help when baby isn't feeling well.

4

Health Care
for Your Baby

Dante has a cold now. I get scared because last time he got sick he had the stomach flu. We had to put him on clear liquids, and give him Pedialyte. That was hard.

When he's sick, you can tell because his eyes look real weak. Now that he has a cold, you can tell because of the snot and the weak eyes, but he still smiles.

Shantika, 17 - Dante, 5 months

Donovan gets sick easy. When he was little, two months old, he had pneumonia, and he was in the hospital for two weeks. I took him to the hospital four times for asthma.

Belia, 17 - Donovan, 2

Her First Doctor's Appointment

Health care is changing. Families may have their health care provided by a doctor, nurse practitioner, a physician's assistant, or other specialist. These people are sometimes referred to as *healthcare providers.* Both "doctor" and "healthcare provider" are used here to mean health professional.

You probably selected your baby's doctor/medical plan before your child was born. Healthcare providers generally have you bring the baby in when she's about two weeks old. At this visit it's good to talk about any troubles at all with feeding. If you have concerns with the baby's navel (belly button), if you suspect hernia, or if you have other worries, tell your healthcare provider.

It's a good idea on your first visit to the healthcare provider to learn the names of the various people working there. If you know the names of the receptionist and the nurse, you can call them by name when you telephone. If you do so, you're more likely to get a friendly response.

Above all, don't be afraid to ask questions. Write down everything you want to discuss with your healthcare provider. Is he always in a hurry? Stop him and say, "Wait. I have these questions, and I need your help."

If you briefly describe whatever is worrying you, he'll take time to advise you. If he doesn't, perhaps you need to look for another doctor who will answer your questions.

You are the case manager for your child's medical needs. Keep all the information together in a notebook so you can grab it when you take your baby to the doctor. Some mothers keep this notebook in the car so they'll have it with them.

Be sure to keep the notebook up to date. If you're in a managed care health plan, you may see a different doctor each time you go. With the notebook, you'll communicate better with the doctor. He will treat you differently because you'll be seen as a capable young mother. That's better for both you and your baby.

Keeping a family health record is important. Start with recording your baby's length and weight at birth and periodically thereafter. If you know your baby's blood type, write it down. Most important is to keep a record of your child's immunizations. You'll have to have this record when he starts to school.

As suggested, write down the dates of your child's illnesses and briefly describe symptoms. This will help you provide information to your healthcare provider and will be a record of this part of your child's development.

Babies and Colic

She had colic when she was little, about two hours at night. I figured out what made her calm. Like about a half-hour into her crying, after carrying her around, I would give her a bath. The water calmed her down.

You have to find what she wants, like finding an itch.

Aimee, 17 - Amelia, 10 months

Some babies cry and cry, and it seems impossible to comfort them. Such a baby may have colic. If he does, he may seem to have a stomach-ache and have attacks of crying nearly every evening. His face may suddenly become red; he'll frown, draw up his legs, and scream loudly. When you pick him up to comfort him, he keeps screaming, perhaps for 15 to 20 minutes. Just as he is about to fall asleep, he may start screaming again. He may pass gas.

No one knows what causes colic. It generally comes at about the same time every day. During the rest of the day, the colicky baby will probably be happy, alert, eat well, and gain weight.

If your baby seems to have colic, check with your doctor to see if anything else is wrong. If not, make sure baby isn't hungry, wet, cold, or lonely. During an attack of colic, holding him on his stomach across your knees may comfort him. Sometimes giving him a warm bath helps. There are also some medicines that may help. Ask your doctor.

The good news about colic is that baby will grow out of it by the time he is about three months old. In the meantime, he will be harder to live with because of his colic. Comfort him as best you can, and look forward to the time his colic ends.

When Lance was a baby, he always had to be held. He was colicky, and we walked with him a lot. Then overnight at about four months he changed, and he was the best little baby. He was happy, and he didn't cry much any more. What a change.

Celia, 20 - Lance, 18 months; Laurel, 4 years

Dealing with Diaper Rash

The best way to deal with diaper rash is to prevent it as much as possible. Change baby during the first month or two before every feeding or more often if he has a bowel movement. Some diapers agree with certain skins better than others, so try all the brands. (Start with the cheaper ones.)

When baby starts sleeping ten to twelve hours at night (such luxury!), put two diapers on her. If she still wets an enormous amount — her clothing and bedding are drenched — you can triple-diaper, using a combination of cloth and disposable diapers.

Change your baby often. Wash her with clean warm water or wipes when you change her. The main cause of diaper rash is the ammonia in the urine coming in contact with air. If she gets a rash, it's even more important to wash her thoroughly each time you change her.

You can put cornstarch or baby powder on her bottom after you take off her wet diaper, but it isn't necessary. If you use baby powder, don't shake it directly on baby. Instead, put a little in your hand first, then pat it on the baby. Baby powder shaken in the air can hurt baby's lungs.

There are both prescription and non-prescription remedies for diaper rash. You can get these either as powder or ointment. During the day the powder is better because, each time you change her, you can wash it off without irritating the rash. At night, however, when baby will sleep longer, use the ointment. It will give longer protection.

If baby has a bad diaper rash, let her go without a diaper as much as possible. If she's warm enough, let her nap without a diaper. The air on the rash will help clear it up. You can protect her bed with waterproof sheeting.

To repeat, it's easier to prevent diaper rash than it is to get rid of it. For your baby's comfort — and your peace of mind — change her often. And clean her thoroughly each time you change her.

Some diaper rashes occur when a baby is taking an antibiotic. Tell your healthcare provider, and she may recommend a special cream to help.

Importance of Immunizations

Sometimes babies are sick. They have colds, fevers, and other illnesses. Later in this chapter, you will find suggestions for dealing with these usually minor illnesses.

There are other serious childhood diseases, diseases that your child need never have. It's up to you because your healthcare provider can immunize him against such diseases.

During the first eighteen months it is important to be sure your baby's immunization schedule is followed. In the past many babies died in the first year or two of life from serious illnesses that now can be prevented by these immunizations.

Here's what your child will need:

• **Hepatitis B** is given in a series of three injections. Usually the first is given on baby's first day after birth, the second at one to two months, and the last one at six months. Baby must have all three.

• **Diphtheria, Tetanus, Pertussis (DTaP)** is also given in a series of three at 2, 4, and 6 months with a booster (Td) at 15-18 months.

• **H. influenzae, type b (Hib)** is another series of three. This is often given in the same injection as the DTaP and is then called HDTaP.

• **Polio (IPV)** is a red liquid given by mouth at two and four months with a third dose given at 6-18 months.

• **Measles, mumps and rubella (MMR)** is given once at 12-15 months.

• **Varicella (chickenpox)** is given once at 12-15 months.

• **Rotavirus (Rv)** is a new vaccine that prevents diarrheal diseases. It is given at two, four, and six months.

• A skin test for **tuberculosis** is usually given at 12-15 months, often at the same time the MMR is given.

Typical Immunization Schedule

At birth: Hepatitis B
2 months: HDTaP; hepatitis B; Rotavirus (Rv); polio
4 months: HDTaP; hepatitis B; Rv; polio
6 months: HDTaP; hepatitis B; Rv; polio (can be
              later, up to 18 months)
12-15 months: MMR, Varicella, TB skin test

While this may seem like a lot for baby, it is important to remember that all of these diseases can cause death or very serious illness in children. When I (Jean B.) was a young nurse, I remember having a baby cough himself to death in my arms from pertussis. I felt especially sad because even then his death could have been prevented if he had just been immunized. *Don't take a chance with your baby!*

It is also *very important* to keep the records of your child's immunizations. If you lose it, get another one right away. When your child starts school, the school will insist on having this information. It may be hard to get it several years later.

Many people keep the immunization card in their child's diaper bag so that if an emergency arises away from home, you can show the information to your healthcare provider.

Immunizations are free at the health department. They may be given by the health department at local parks. If

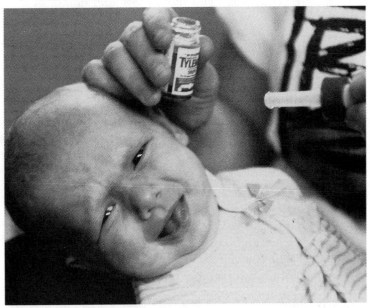

If she has a fever, the doctor may prescribe a non-aspirin pain reliever.

you don't know where to take your baby for his shots, ask
your school nurse for a recommendation.

Possible Reaction to Shots

*When Nick got his shots, he got a lot of fever —
that really bothered him. He woke up at midnight with
a fever, and I gave him Tylenol. That helped.*

Theresa, 16 - Nick, 6 months

Most babies have some reaction to immunizations.
Usually the reaction lasts only a day or two and is generally
mild. Giving your child a baby non-aspirin pain reliever
such as Tylenol or Pediacare will help relieve these
symptoms. See page 70 for suggestions about caring for a
feverish child.

Of course, if your baby has a severe reaction to his
immunizations (high fever for more than twelve hours or
other severe symptoms), you should call your doctor.

Be sure to keep a record of your baby's immunizations.
You will need these records to enroll your child in school.

When Should You Call Your Doctor?

*You call the doctor when you don't know what to
do because there's something wrong with the baby.
He might get upset if you overdo it — mine did once,
but better safe than sorry.*

*Sometimes, if I'm worried but don't think there's
much wrong, I go to another mother before I call the
doctor. If Robin has a fever or seems sick, I call.*

Melinda, 15 - Robin, 9 months

When should you call your baby's healthcare provider?
If you take baby's temperature under his arm (less disturb-
ing to the baby than is sticking a thermometer into his
rectum), and it reads more than 101 degrees, call.

The best way to take underarm (called axillary) temperature is with a disposable or digital thermometer. These are available in drugstores. If possible, use them to take baby's temperature. Otherwise, use a glass thermometer.

If your baby gets a sudden unexplained rash, call your healthcare provider.

Many babies spit up occasionally during the first two months. This is generally a combination of lumps of partially digested milk combined with watery-looking fluid. They do this because their digestive tract is not completely mature. This happens more often with premature babies. He will spit up less if you give him frequent small feedings and handle him extra gently after feeding.

Generally, this occasional spitting up is nothing to worry about. But if baby, after every feeding, suddenly vomits most of his meal, call his healthcare provider immediately.

Before you call your doctor, make some notes about your baby's condition. Then you'll be able to describe his symptoms more accurately:

- Is he coughing? For how long?
- Has he lost his appetite?
- Does he have diarrhea?
- What is his temperature?
- Has he been exposed to any diseases? Has he received the immunizations he should have had by this time?

If your healthcare provider prescribes medication for your baby, be sure to ask if you should give baby all the medicine that's in the bottle, or if you give it only for a certain number of days. Most antibiotics (Penicillin, Ampicillin, Ilison) need to be used until they are all gone. However, decongestants such as Actifed and Dimetapp are to be used only when symptoms of congestion are present — when he has a stuffy, runny nose.

Diarrhea Can Be Serious

Diarrhea, which can be a serious problem for a baby, is not diagnosed by the number of bowel movements the baby has each day. More important is the consistency of the BM.

Diarrhea: a thin, watery, foul-smelling discharge

If baby has this condition for as long as twelve hours, call the healthcare provider. A baby with diarrhea can quickly lose a dangerous amount of fluid.

Diarrhea is best treated by giving the baby clear liquids and nothing else for 24 hours. Liquids you should give him include Pedialyte (non-prescription liquid you buy in the drugstore or grocery store), clear water, or water mixed with apple juice (one tablespoon apple juice to 8 ounces of water). Offer no solid foods, and feed him liquids as often as he'll take them.

Hernia? Check with Doctor

If you think your baby might have a hernia, check with your healthcare provider.

Hernia: a bulge around the navel or the seamline between the leg and the tummy

---

You're most likely to notice it after baby has cried a lot or strained to have a bowel movement. Sometimes it will go away by itself, but occasionally it requires simple surgery. If your doctor recommends surgery, it's usually done during the second year of baby's life.

Dealing with Fever

Fever is one of the early signs of illness in a baby, and you shouldn't ignore it. What can you do about fever at

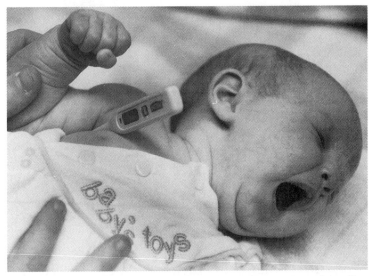

Taking underarm temperature with a digital thermometer works well.

home? Give the baby Tylenol or other non-aspirin pain reliever as recommended by your doctor.

Cooling baths are another way to bring fever down. If baby shivers while you're bathing him, it's too cold. A good way to do this is to put a towel in lukewarm water. Then wrap the baby in the wet towel. It helps bring his temperature down, and he's less likely to shiver.

Lukewarm water is the best thing to use. Don't use alcohol. The fumes can be dangerous for baby to breathe.

It's also important to give your child liquids when he has a fever. If it's a sore throat that's causing his fever, your baby may not want to do a lot of sucking.

That one throat infection Lynn had was terrible. I took her to the doctor, and they gave me Penicillin to give her. About a week later I took her back to school.

She was really sick — she couldn't keep anything down. She couldn't suck the bottle because her throat was so sore. She cried a lot. We'd go to sleep, and

*she'd wake up 15 minutes later. Her crying got on my
nerves, but when I picked her up, she'd quit crying.*
Sheryl Ann, 17 - Lynn, 7 months

A way to encourage your child to take lots of liquids is
to give him popsicles. If a little piece breaks off in his
mouth, it will melt quickly and he can swallow it. This
much sugar won't hurt him. Popsicles are also good for babies and toddlers if they have a lot of nausea and vomiting.
Sucking on a popsicle will often help. You can freeze fruit
juices to make your own popsicles if you don't want to buy
the sugary ones. Besides being cold and making him feel
better, homemade juicesicles are nutritious.

Ear Infection? Call Doctor

*Jonita had an ear infection which made her congestion
problem even worse. Yes, I used to prop bottles. My mom
probably still props them.*
Ellen, 17 - Jonita, 6 months

When your child has an ear infection, call your healthcare provider. While a non-aspirin pain reliever can take
away some of the pain and the fever, it doesn't kill the
germs causing the infection in the ear.

On one of your first visits, ask the doctor what to do if
your baby gets an ear infection. Some healthcare providers
want to see the baby right away. Others may recommend
some things you can try first such as a decongestant. Do
whatever is recommended but don't ignore this illness.

As discussed in chapter 2, many infants' ear infections
are caused by propped bottles.

Colds Are Common

Most children catch a few colds during their first two
years. Colds are most contagious the first couple of days,

sometimes before the carrier knows he's sick, so it's impossible to protect your child completely from getting colds.

When Evan was three weeks old, he caught his first cold. Marlene kept a record of those days:

> *9/4: Today Evan has a slight cough. I hope it doesn't get worse.*
>
> *9/5: Evan got the sniffles and his cough is worse. When I feed him, he'll cough, and it seems like he's choking. It scares me.*
>
> *9/6: Evan's cold is getting worse. His nose is plugged. I called the doctor, and she told me to use normal saline and put it in his nose because he has a hard time breathing. I'm gonna take him to the doctor tomorrow because I want to make sure. My mom is helping me out.*
>
> *9/8: Today Evan woke up around 9:00 and slept through most of the day. He's still coughing. His sniffles are getting a little better but he still gets plugged up from time to time. During the night, as usual, he's a grouch, but I finally got him to sleep by holding him in my arms and singing to him like I usually do.*
>
> *9/9: Evan is a month old. He stays awake a lot. I don't mind that. It's the crying I could live without.*
>
> *9/10: 1 wish his cold would go away. The doctor said we can't give him any medication because he's too young. I feel so sorry for him because it seems like he's having such a hard time.*
>
> *9/12: He's still sick. He stays up so much, and he's always crying. I hate his cold. I don't have time these past few days to do anything because he's always awake and crying because he doesn't feel good.*
>
> *9/14: Finally he's feeling better.*

Neither you nor your healthcare provider can "cure" your child's cold — there is no known cure. You can help him be more comfortable. If he has a fever or headache, Tylenol may help.

If he has a runny or stuffy nose, use normal saline and a rubber syringe to clean the discharge from baby's nose. Normal saline is available from the drugstore without a prescription. The hospital probably gave you a rubber syringe for this purpose for baby.

Decongestant medicine may also make him feel better. If his nose is sore, cream or ointment on the area is soothing.

If he's coughing, your doctor may recommend cough medicine. If he has a stuffy nose, a cold-water vaporizer will help him breathe more easily. The old-fashioned steam vaporizers are dangerous, and they don't work as well.

If he doesn't want to eat, don't worry. When he's feeling better, he'll be hungry again. Encourage him to drink juice, water, clear soups, even a little weak tea.

How often your child has a cold depends on two things: the number of people with colds to whom he is exposed, and his own resistance.

If he's in good health generally, eats nutritious meals instead of junk foods, and gets plenty of rest, he is much less likely to get sick.

He May Have an Allergy

Stuffy noses can be due to allergies. Allergies are caused generally by reactions to foods, plants, animals, or pollutants. A large percentage of allergies in children under two seem to be caused by food so doctors generally recommend changes in diet for babies with these symptoms.

If a mother smokes during pregnancy, her baby is at greater risk for developing asthma and other allergies. When an infant or child breathes second-hand smoke, it can have the same effect. A smoke-free home is a wonderful gift to give your child. Not having to breathe smoke means he's less likely to get sick with a respiratory problem.

A lot of allergies disappear in time as baby becomes more adjusted to life on the outside. Therefore, most doctors don't start serious allergy testing until a child is much older, usually school age.

Caution — Sick Child

If your baby has something like conjunctivitis (pink eye) or impetigo (skin infection), you shouldn't have him around other children. You should take the same precautions during the first day or two he has a cold.

If you know a friend's child has one of these conditions, keep your baby away from him. Of course, later when your child is out in the neighborhood playing, he will pick up an illness occasionally because you can't control your neighbor's child. These generally aren't serious diseases. Mainly they're an annoyance to both you and your child that you avoid if you can.

Keeping your baby as healthy as possible is one of the challenges of parenthood. First, do all you can to insure she has a good diet, gets plenty of sleep, and receives other good physical care in addition to an unending supply of love.

When she doesn't feel well, call your healthcare provider. Help her be as comfortable as possible. Hopefully, she will soon be her happy, active self again.

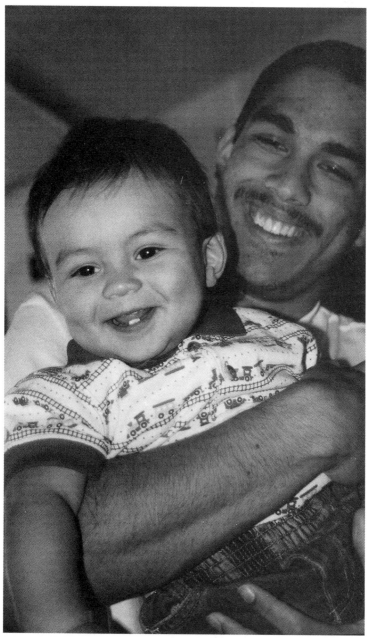

Dad is very special to him.

5

For Dad Only

I was scared when she told me she was pregnant. I was working, but I didn't know how I was going to support her and the baby. I couldn't even support myself. I was also real excited. I was happy but I was scared.

Katlia was scared, too. We were in this together.

I knew everything was going to be different. Nothing would ever be the same again. I felt like my freedom was going to be taken away. I couldn't come and go as I pleased, but I wanted to do the right thing. I wanted my daughter to have a father.

Raul, 19 - Elena, 23 months

*The first time I had to change him was an experi-
ence I won't forget. I had never changed a baby
before. It was weird because I never had to watch
over anyone, something so small that was mine.
Before I hadn't even worried about myself, and now I
have to give him a lot of my attention.*

Andy, 17 - Gus, 5 months (Yolanda, 15)

*We shared the night feedings. Luckily Dustin
started sleeping through the night real soon. We did it
all together.*

*I don't think it would be fair if I just said I'm not
getting up, I'm not going to give him a bottle. We
shared the responsibility of having him. I think you
have to go 50-50.*

Mark, 22 - Dustin, 2 1/2

Many teen mothers parent their child alone. This book is
written for them. It is *also* written for:

• Young couples who are parenting their child together.

• Young fathers who are involved with their child, or
   would like to be, whether or not they are still "with"
   their child's mother.

• Teen fathers who are parenting alone.

While most of these chapters are written to all teenage
parents, this chapter is especially for fathers. Chapter 6
focuses on the special needs of mothers parenting alone.

If you're a teen father (or an older father) and you're
reading this book, obviously you don't fit the stereotype of
the teen father who gets his girlfriend pregnant, then takes
no responsibility for his family. Whether you're married,
living with your baby's mother, or not living with her, you
probably are taking an important role in rearing your child.

If you and your baby's mother aren't married, it's

important that you "establish paternity." This means that you both sign legal papers stating that you are the father of your child. If you don't, your child might not be able to claim Social Security, insurance benefits, veteran's and other types of benefits through you.

Your child needs your love and care. He also needs your financial support. Both parents are required by law to support their child.

Sharing Care of Your Newborn

Mario feeds Carol, changes her, and plays with her. He even got up to feed her last night. He put her in her crib, and she started crying. So he picked her up and put her next to him, and she fell asleep. I'm glad she's like that. I'm glad she's attached to her dad.

Mario wanted to go fishing the other night. I said if it was cold, the baby and I would stay home. He went outside and decided it was warm enough, so we all went to the lake. He caught a fish and showed it to little Carol.

Let the baby get close to her father. It's really neat.

Kristyn, 17 - Carol, 3 months

Fathers often get deeply involved in child care. Your baby probably is a charming little person much of the time. Caring for him can be rewarding for you and for him. In fact, this can be a very special relationship for father and baby.

The play between a father and his baby tends to be quite active and generally includes a lot of talk. It can be especially exciting to the baby. Along with the activity, he enjoys the lower pitch of his father's voice. Even at a very early age, conversation between father and baby will occur quite easily. The father says words and baby responds with

various sounds and facial expressions. In some families,
babies look to mother for nurturing and comfort and look
forward to excitement and fun with dad. Both parents play
a special role with their child.

Who Gets Up with Baby?

*Night feedings? Diaper changings? I tried to help
her, but I guess I really wasn't that great with me
going to work. I was kind of a grouch getting up at 3
a.m. It was a lot of stress although Elena was a good
baby. She got up more at night later.*

*The first month Elena would mostly sleep, but later
when she got up she wouldn't want to go back to bed.
It was hard for me to get back to sleep, too. I'd get up
early and go to work, and I'd be exhausted. Gradually
she started sleeping through the night.*

*On weekends I tried to spend as much time with
Elena as I could, but I had to work a lot of overtime in
order for us to manage. I remember working fourteen*

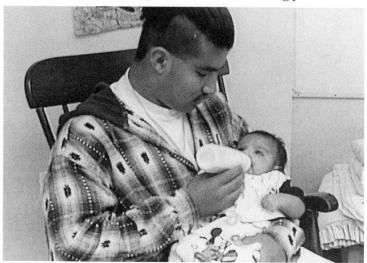

It's his turn to get up with baby tonight.

hours a day, and it wasn't a choice. I had to. I couldn't miss a day. Even when Elena was born at 5 a.m., after she was born, I went to work.

Raul

If dad is working and mom is home with the baby, they may agree on a traditional separation of work with mom taking care of the baby most of the time. Even then, having a tiny baby in the house, one who is awake and crying much of the night, makes it hard for mom to get enough rest and for dad to get enough sleep to be alert at his job the next day.

Many teenage parents, however, don't have the luxury of one parent being home full-time with baby. Both mom and dad may be in school, and both may also have a job. Expecting mom to care for the baby by herself is not very rational. Caring for a baby takes a lot of energy. When mom and dad share the work, they are more likely to share the joys of parenting.

Rene and Greg weren't living together when Vanessa was born. Greg was 19 and appeared pleased about the pregnancy. He worked part-time the first year, and Rene continued to live with her mother. Because he didn't live with his child, he wasn't much involved in baby care. When Vanessa was nine months old, Rene moved in with Greg. Now they have a second baby, and Rene reports that Greg is much more involved:

During the week I get up with the baby because Greg has to leave early in the morning, but on the weekends he gets up at night. This was the deal we made before Shavone was born.

We weren't living together when Vanessa was born, and Greg kept complaining that he missed out on a lot with her. We talked it over when I was

*pregnant again — about the things he would do and
what I would do. It's working pretty well.*

Rene, 18 - Vanessa, 19 months; Shavone, 1 month

If You Don't Live with Your Baby

You may have a close relationship with your baby's
mother even if you're not living together. Perhaps you took
prepared childbirth classes together. You may have been
deeply involved coaching mother through labor and delivery. Perhaps you're caring for the baby as much as you can.

If baby's parents are not married, how much "should"
father be included? If the young family lives together, they
probably feel much the same about joint parenting as do
married couples. If they don't live together, there is no
pattern cut and ready for them to follow. Dad can still play
an important role in his baby's life.

Shaun was away at college Monday through Thursday
each week during the first months after his baby's birth. He
spent weekends at his parents' home about three miles from
Beth Ann who lived with her parents. Troy didn't sleep a
lot during his first two months, and Beth Ann, 17, was
exhausted. Shaun decided he could help:

*I'm very involved with Troy. I take him overnight
once a week to give Beth Ann a break so she can
catch up on her sleep. This way, I get to be with Troy.
My mom or my sister help some, but I do most of it.
For some reason, he has trouble sleeping at Beth
Ann's house, but with me, he takes his bottle, eats,
plays, and goes to bed. He sleeps five or six hours. I
wish he'd do that for Beth Ann.*

Shaun, 19 - Troy, 2 months

It's possible that Troy senses more stress at his mother's
house. It's also possible that having him only once a week

means Shaun has more energy to play with him. Babies sense how a parent feels. If the parent is upset, baby probably is, too. If the parent relaxes, baby may do the same thing.

If you aren't with your baby's mother, you can still have a relationship with your child. Unless the court forbids it, you have a right to see your child and to spend time with her. Even if you aren't able to provide for her financially at this point, share your time.

Work out an arrangement so that your baby's mother also has some free time. Too often, the young mother is saddled with the entire responsibility of caring for the baby while the father doesn't even get to see his child. When this happens, everyone loses.

How Do Mom's Parents Feel?

Mother and baby may live with mother's parents. Her parents may have firm opinions about how much, if at all, the young father should be involved. This can be a difficult situation for everyone.

If Yolanda goes home and stays with her parents, I can't go over there and see my baby. When she's here, most of the time we take turns taking care of him. Yolanda isn't in school, so after school I go home and take care of him so she can sleep. Sometimes I have him on the weekends, sometimes she does. We take turns going out —most of the time if we stay at the house together, we end up fighting.

Andy

Yolanda and Andy are under a lot of stress. Her parents still don't like Andy, and Yolanda is not happy living at Andy's house. They need to talk about their feelings, work through this stage, and know that they may feel less stressed when Gus is a little older. It takes a lot of effort, determination, and love to make a relationship work at any age. It may be especially hard when the partners are teenagers who already have a baby.

What About Marriage?

We waited for marriage because I wanted to make sure it was right. I didn't want to end up with a divorce when he was 5 or so and put him through that trauma. My dad skipped out on me, and I didn't want to put my kid through what I went through. We didn't want to rush into it. Her parents were real stressed out, and they were trying to plan a wedding for us, but no, no, we didn't want to go.

Chris, 20 - Alex, 12 months

He has a special relationship with his dad.

What about marriage? Should you marry *because* you're having a child together? Getting married just because of the pregnancy probably isn't a good idea. It's too easy for the partners to blame each other when things get difficult later. For this and other reasons, some couples choose to delay marriage.

Chris and Erin were married when Alex was five months old. Now Chris has a fairly good job and they have their own little apartment, but it still isn't easy. Chris continued:

> *I have a lot of responsibility now. I feel a lot of stress. I'm 20 years old and I feel like I'm 40. We go shopping and the baby gets this and Erin gets that, and there may be $3 left for socks for me.*

New Baby Hard on Relationships

> *I was never good with babies, but Keonia made me understand babies' needs. Before she was born, my husband and I were very close, but now we've drifted apart and we seldom talk to each other anymore. We argue more than usual.*
>
> *Keonia makes me feel like I'm 30 years old. I feel I'm not a little girl anymore or a carefree teenager. A lot of times I feel that I'm giving all my love to my daughter and there isn't any left for my husband.*
>
> Lei, 16 - Keonia, 4 months

Many couples find that the stress of caring for a baby combined with money problems is hard on their relationship. Lei and Roy were married a month before Keonia was born. Keonia has had medical problems including two brief stays in the hospital. Lei takes most of the responsibility for her care while Roy leaves early in the morning for work and doesn't get back until after 6:00.

Hopefully Lei and Roy are able to talk about their relationship and make a conscious effort to regain their closeness. They may want to discuss their relationship with a counselor before they drift further apart.

Sometimes the father feels left out because mom appears to know more about caring for their baby than he does.

*It's brought us together but it's different because
now Brooke feels it's more of a thing, "I'm the
mother, I've been with him." It's more "I" than
"We." That bothers me. It irks me to the point that I
get downright mad.*

*Brooke acts as if I'm the babysitter, I'm not his
father. She finally lets me change him and feed him.
At first she hovered over me like I didn't know what I
was doing and like she had raised so many kids. All
she had done was help people out, she hadn't
raised them.*

Joel, 19 - Blair, 3 months

Probably the best thing for Joel to do is become an
expert himself. He's far more than the babysitter, and he
knows it. He and Brooke need to talk through these feelings. Probably Brooke will become a little less nervous,
and, therefore, less bossy as Blair gets a little older. One
thing is sure — nobody would win if Joel decided to quit
caring for his son because he thinks the mother isn't as
positive as he'd like.

Making Time for Partner

*I felt a little left out at first after Genny was born,
but I never said anything about it. I felt guilty, too,
when I felt like that. I got over it quick.*

Miguel, 21 - Genny, 18 months

Sometimes a new father feels left out because his partner
seems to give all of her time and attention to the baby.
Mom can have some of those feelings, too:

*He's very involved with her. In fact, he forgets all
about me. He walks through the door and goes
straight to her. I'll say, "Remember me?"*

He plays with her, feeds her, changes her diaper,

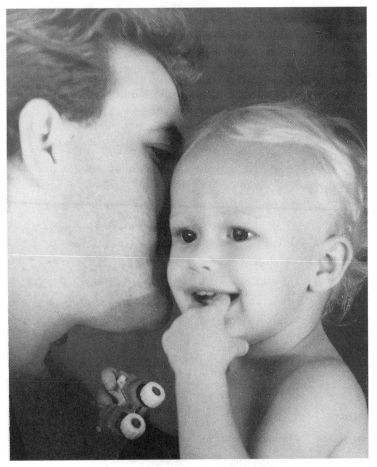

He's listening while Dad whispers in his ear.

*everything. She looks like him. He's 23, and I'm 16.
He wasn't working when I got pregnant, but I think
the responsibility hit him. He got a job and we're fine.*

Marsha, 16 - Justin, 5 months

You and your partner may find it's hard to make time for each other when you have a new baby. It's important for your baby's sake as well as your own that both of you continue to work toward a stronger and stronger relationship.

Financial Problems May Occur

Financial problems tend to be intense for many teenage couples. Even if dad has a job, the money probably won't stretch as far as they'd like. Chris, like many young fathers, works so hard supporting his family that he has little time to spend with his son:

> *When Alex was born I was only making $5 an hour, but I was determined this kid would be all right. I'd get two jobs if I had to.*
>
> *I didn't have a chance to discuss my feelings. I was on my own from the time I was 16. I left home. I didn't need anybody, and I was living pretty bad. I was living on the streets.*
>
> *I met Erin, and she kind of straightened me out. I got a job and tried to do something better with my life. I think it might have helped to talk with other young fathers, hear how they cope.*
>
> *I don't get to see much of Alex. I leave here at 5:30 a.m., and get home at 7:30, so I see him for less than an hour each evening. On the weekends we spend time together.*

School Is Important

If you're still in school, you probably can't support your family by yourself. Most important for you right now is to graduate and acquire job skills so you can become independent as soon as possible. Many young parents continue to live with their parents until they're ready to be self-supporting. Andy is struggling to finish school. Because there is no one else to care for their child, Yolanda is enrolled in independent study. Andy talked about their life together:

I want Gus to grow good. I don't want him to be in the streets or nothing. I'm going to try to teach him what's right and what's wrong. I don't want him to grow up like I did or like my brothers.

We have our difficult times. Yolanda gets those weird ideas when we don't have enough money and we have to save for milk and diapers. Or when he's up crying at night, and I have to go to school. Most of the time when I'm up all night with Gus because he's sick, that's putting off my graduation.

When I go to school Yolanda mostly stays with Gus during the day. Last week she got sick, too, and I had to take care of both of them. Last week I was at school only one day because both of them were sick.

My mom and dad help me out a lot, but that's why I want to get out — so they won't have to worry about my baby.

Other guys — I'd tell them to wait until they're through with school and have a job. It's hard with no money. It's hard trying to go to school with the baby whether you're a mother or a father.

If you're already a father, you know that handling your responsibility is hard. Hopefully, you also know the *joys* that come along with those parenting responsibilities. Spend time with your child. You can be an extremely important part of his life.

For further information, see **Teen Dads: Rights, Responsibilities and Joys** *by Lindsay (Morning Glory).*

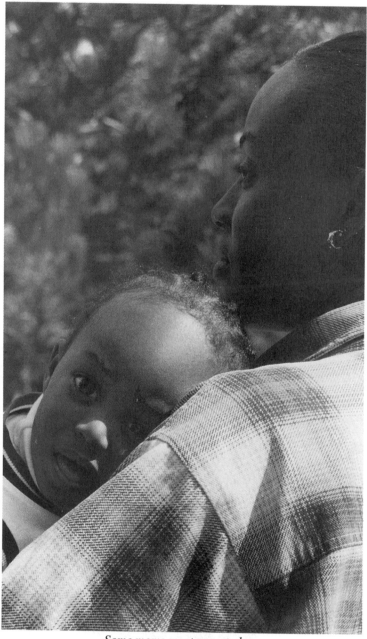

Some moms must parent alone.

6

If Mom
Is Alone

I would feel even more alone if the father had been with me through-out pregnancy, then left. But he left three months after I got pregnant. I'm not in touch with him at all. He's entirely out of the picture.

Sometimes I see a friend with her boyfriend and baby, and wish Orlando had a father. But other times I wonder if I'd want to share!

Holly, 17 - Orlando, 5 months

I was fine all through my preg-nancy except the last couple of months were real hard on me. It was stressful. I think it was because I was worrying about a lot of stuff.

Her father and I were together off and on for a while but we didn't talk much. I would call him to tell him how the baby was, and he wouldn't call me. Was he going to be in the baby's life? It's stressful right now because he says he wants to see the baby but he doesn't come over. I'm not pressuring him to come see her. He's almost 18, and he's in school, too.

I would like to be with him but I don't think that it would work. He's the type of person who chooses his friends over other people. He goes out a lot with them and he doesn't make time with the baby. Maybe later. His friends have been in a gang and he hangs around with them.

Lacey, 16 - Jenilee, 1 month

About five out of six teenage mothers are not married when they give birth. Some of these young mothers are quite alone. The baby's father may have left when he learned of the pregnancy. In some cases, he may not even know about the baby:

It makes it hard being the father and mother at the same time. It would help to have a father around, but there is nothing I can do about it. When Pedro grows up, I don't know what I'll tell him. His father never knew I was pregnant. I put "unknown" on the birth certificate.

My big brother is around, and he holds him. I think that will help.

Maria, 17 - Pedro, 2 months

Maria had a tough time for three years. She lived at home, and managed to go to school fairly regularly. When Pedro was three, Maria married Ralph (not Pedro's father). They now have four children including Pedro.

The fact that your child's father is not around doesn't mean your child will never have a father. A "real" father is a dad who is actively parenting. Ralph is Pedro's real father because he is the one who has taken that role.

On Being Positive — and Honest

Do I Have a Daddy? by Lindsay (1991: Morning Glory Press) is a picture book for the child who doesn't know his biological father. Included in the book is a section of suggestions for a single mother. Young mothers share their thoughts on this important topic. These young mothers stress two things:

• Be honest with your child.
• Be as positive as possible.

For some young mothers, these goals are in conflict. Perhaps at this point you find it hard to say anything good about your child's father. Raylene is in this position:

I thought maybe because Rick is his dad, I should give marriage a thought. But I knew I would be getting into the same abuse my mom is in except Rick didn't drink. He was mean when he was sober, while my dad does it when he's drunk. I didn't even consider marrying him.

Rick would say, "You'll never find anybody else. Guys will think you're a whore." The last time he hit me was six weeks before Victor was born. I realized I deserved better. I would rather be alone and single forever than put up with that.

Raylene 18 - Victor, 2

Talking in a positive way with Victor about his father will be hard for Raylene. However, in *Do I Have a Daddy?* Robin says:

*Why make a kid feel like his father was a louse? If
his dad's a louse, that makes him half-louse. It's not
fair to lay your feelings on your child.*
  *I tell Stu, "Your father wasn't as lucky as I am —
he didn't get to live with you.*

                                        Robin, 21 - Stu, 5

Robin is right. It's important for your child's sake that
you try to look beyond your own feelings. This will be
difficult for Raylene. She may decide to level with Victor
at some time and tell him that she and his father had a very
poor relationship. With the passage of time, perhaps she
will also be able to share some positive memories with
her son.

Filing for Child Support

*I want to get full custody of my daughter. I want to
make sure that he won't take her from me later on. I
feel very sad and disappointed because he says he
cares about my daughter and that he wants to see her
all the time, but he has only been able to see her three
times. We live only five blocks away from each other,
but he doesn't find the time to come see her. His mom
comes to see her all the time but he doesn't.*

                                        Lacey, 16 – Jenilee, 1 month

Lacey isn't sure she wants to file for child support. Some
young mothers choose not even to name the father of their
baby. They don't file for child support. "I can do it on my
own," they say.
  This isn't fair to the child. Even if the father has no job
and no money now and you don't think you want your
child to know him, it's still important that he not be shut
out of his child's life forever.

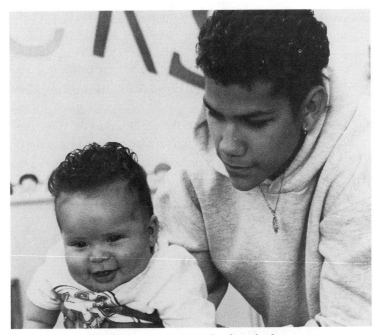

Your child has a right to benefits from both parents.

Both parents are required by law to support their child,
whether or not they planned to have a child together. A
child supported by only one parent is likely to be poor. He
has a right to benefits from both parents, benefits such as
Social Security, insurance benefits, inheritance rights,
veteran's and other benefits. You need to establish paternity so that your child will be able to claim such benefits.
In some states, paternity is established by both mother and
father signing a legal paper saying he is the father.

If the father refuses to admit paternity, you may need to
go to court. Blood tests are almost 100 percent accurate in
identifying the father of a child. The blood tests are genetic
tests which compare many different factors in your blood
with similar parts of the man's and the child's blood.

Some couples are close throughout much of the

pregnancy, then split up before the baby is born. Kellie's situation is typical:

> *We aren't together now but Ron's paying child support. He hasn't seen Kevin since he was a month old.*
>
> *We had been together for two years, and we were close up to my eighth month. He was excited about the whole thing. Then Ron's parents separated and his brother was getting divorced. He got scared that would happen to us.*
>
> *Ron was back with me for about a month after Kevin was born, then left again. Now he's trying to come back. I'm not going to let that happen because I don't want Kevin hurt again, and I don't want to be hurt.*
>
> *We had talked of marriage. Then in just one week we went from planning marriage to he never wanted to see me again. I think he's scared of growing up and taking responsibility.*
>
> *I wouldn't think it was possible, but Ron's feelings seemed to change overnight. I think it had a lot to do with his mother. Once I got pregnant, she went totally against me. I was fine, good enough for him until I got pregnant. Then she decided I was trying to trap him. We had a good relationship those two years. We hardly ever fought.*
>
> Kellie, 16 - Kevin, 3 months

It's impossible to say what Kellie "should" do. It's possible that she and Ron will eventually decide to parent together — or they may not. In either case, Kellie is wise to have filed for child support. She also may decide, even if she and Ron are not together, that Ron and Kevin need to have a relationship.

Other People's Comments

Being alone during pregnancy and afterward is extremely difficult for many moms. Other people may make it even harder:

When you see someone with the father, you just want to cry because you aren't going to have a father for your baby. I'd hear all of these girls talking about the baby's father, and how we aren't together.

They would ask me questions like "Are you with the baby's father? Are you going to get married?" You have to answer them, and it's embarrassing. Sometimes you want to cry right then. Sometimes they know they brought up a sad subject and will try to talk about something else.

Goldie, 17 - Jimmy, 3 months

You *don't* "have to answer them." It's okay to say, "I'd rather not talk about it." You don't owe people an explanation. On the other hand, sometimes it helps to talk about our problems with someone we trust. When you're parenting alone, having the support of a few close friends can help a lot.

Having friends is also important if you're with your baby's father. Maurine stayed with Miguel for more than a year after Genny was born. She and Miguel were close, so close that Maurine says she gave up her own identity for awhile. She feels now that this was a mistake:

Girls need to learn not to be so dependent. I became terribly dependent on Miguel. Then we'd break up and I'd think I couldn't do anything for myself. You have to be responsible for yourself. It's hard to explain. You think he's everything.

Until they have experienced it, a lot of girls aren't

going to believe it could happen to them. That's what
I thought. He was so good to me.

You need to have contact with your friends. I
didn't. I stopped going out with them and stayed with
Miguel because he got so jealous. It's better if you go
out with your friends and he goes out with his. We
were together too much.

I tell him I don't want to get back with him, but he
doesn't want to hear that. That day when we broke up
I felt different. I felt totally free. I like the way I feel.

Maurine, 16 - Genny, 18 months

Dependency is not a good foundation for a relationship.
Maurine and Miguel may get back together, or they may
not. In either case, Maurine's new-found freedom to be
herself is likely to help her build a better relationship in the
future, whether that relationship is with Miguel or with
someone else.

"I Still Like Him"

Beth has very mixed feelings about her child's father:

At first Al saw the baby about every other day, or
called up to see how she was. Then I decided I didn't
want him to see Patty any more. I told him, and we
argued about it. He has the right, I know, and he
really does care about her. I had thought he was the
type of guy who would say, "So I have a baby, so
what?" but he's not.

Al had planned to coach me during labor, then we
started arguing. The subject wasn't brought up again.
I found another coach, a friend of mine.

I haven't seen Al much for quite awhile. When I
was first pregnant, we were going to get married. But
I didn't want to get married just because of the

pregnancy —I think that's a big mistake. Maybe when he works out what he wants to do with his life. . .

Perhaps the real reason I don't want him to see Patty is because I still like him. When he's around here I get really upset. So maybe if/when I don't have these feelings, it will be the right time for him to come around.

Now I still care for him a lot, and when I see him with his daughter, I feel sad. I wish things could have worked out. I know he has the right to see her, but I'm not ready for it, that's all.

Beth, 18 - Patty, 3 weeks

If the baby's father is providing some financial support, and sometimes even if he's not, he has a right to see his baby. Legally, he may be able to have his child with him part of the time. If the young parents disagree on this matter, they should talk to a lawyer or legal aid group.

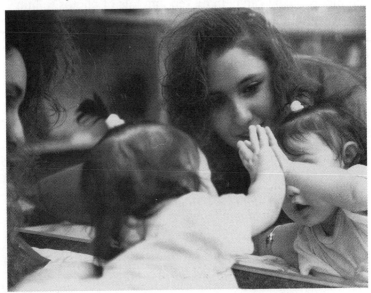

A single parent can certainly be a loving, "good" parent.

Dad May Be Far Away

Sometimes the baby's father can't be with his family. He may be in the armed forces, or he may be away for other reasons:

Jayme has seen his dad once. I took him to the prison when he was 6 months old. I felt very uncomfortable with Cory, and so did Jayme.

It was difficult for me because Cory looked different, his attitude was different, and I was different. I didn't feel as though we had conceived this child together.

Kaylene, 18 – Jayme, 16 months

What is Kaylene's responsibility to Jayme and to Jayme's father? Should she try to maintain a relationship with him? That's a hard question, one that only Kaylene and Cory can answer. If Cory is to have a relationship with Jayme, Kaylene can help by sending lots of photos to him and keeping him up to date on his son's development.

Handling Future Relationships

I've been alone since I was three weeks pregnant, but I've been seeing somebody else for about two months. Jayme loves my new friend. He's starting to notice people are around a lot more, and he gets real attached to people fast. He's used to just me being around, but he's definitely getting into Mommy being with someone else. He likes being a family.

I hadn't dated much before that. I had dated once but that didn't work out because the man I was seeing didn't like kids. He didn't want to be a daddy or anything close, so I ended that real fast.

Kaylene

Young mothers who are alone may wonder how to handle future relationships. How soon should you tell a new friend about your child? Most moms agree that it's important to be honest.

"If he doesn't want to have anything to do with me because I have a baby, he's not for me," they say. On the other hand, sometimes a new boyfriend seems too eager to be a father to the child:

> *Dating other people is hard. I dated one person who liked me, but he thought the only reason I wanted to go out with him was for him to be a father to Kevin. Another one was already putting money away for his college.*
>
> *Finding the right person is going to be hard. It's going to have its ups and downs. I want to find somebody who's not afraid, but who doesn't want to take over the whole situation.*
>
> Kellie

Finding the "right" approach to future relationships can be difficult. You might like your child to have an acting father. At the same time you don't want her to assume that every man who comes around is going to be her dad. When you have a child, handling dating and your relationship with a possible future partner takes a great deal of wisdom, love, and caring.

Single Parenting Can Work

About half the children in the United States today will spend at least part of their lives in a one-parent household. Most people still think it's better for a child to have two parents who care about each other. But a single parent can certainly be a loving, "good" parent. It just takes a little more effort.

Time with Grandma is very special.

7

Three-Generation Living

- Help from Grandma
- "Who's My Mother?"
- Role of Brothers and Sisters
- Key — Taking Responsibility
- Moving in with Partner's Family
- Will Everyone Agree?

I could babysit easily, but when it came to my baby, I needed my mom. She was too bossy, but I did need her. I wish she could have sometimes asked me instead of telling me what to do.

Mom thinks her way is much better because she's older. But I'm a mother, too, and I think I should try my way to see if it works.

If I were living on my own, I think I'd be a nervous wreck. I wouldn't have anyone to ask for advice. But there are times when I want to try something myself because I want to be the responsible person.

Holly, 17 - Orlando, 5 months

Help from Grandma

*When I came home from the hospital, sometimes
I'd feel scared. I didn't know what to do. I was even
scared to carry Racquelle. When she cried and cried,
I cried myself because I didn't know what was wrong.*

Cheryl, 15 - Racquelle, 2 months

Teenage parents, married as well as single, are more
likely to live with their parents than is an older family. How
does this change their approach to baby care and child
rearing?

On the positive side, it is often reassuring as well as less
tiring to have some help with baby care. New parents may
suddenly feel they don't know how to take care of this
small creature. Having your mother in the same house can
be reassuring. During the early weeks of night feeding, she
may even be willing to take an occasional turn at getting up
with the baby while you sleep.

*She loves me and she loves the baby, but the baby
is my responsibility. A couple of times Sonja would
wake up at night and cry and cry. I would cry, too,
and Mom would come in and help. But I want Sonja to
know me as her mother.*

Julie, 16 - Sonja, 7 months

If baby's father isn't around, you may need more help
from grandma. Many young mothers who live with their
parents find the first couple of months with a baby somewhat of a "honeymoon" period. Your parents may be eager
to help you.

If you have brothers and sisters, they may fight over who
gets to hold the baby next. Appreciate their help even as
you do as much as possible for your baby.

"Who's My Mother?"

The neat thing about grandmas is that they're experienced. They've learned from their mistakes. They take time, and have learned how to be patient with a fussy baby.

The not-so-good news is that sometimes grandparents take on too much responsibility. They may appear to forget who the mom is.

If grandmother takes over in the beginning, it may be hard for baby's own mother to take charge later. The result in many families is a baby who thinks grandma is her mother. Baby's mother then feels left out and resentful. Most hurt may be baby who isn't sure who mother really is.

I catch my mother occasionally playing the mother role. I can understand that because she has the experience. Besides, I really need that when I'm tired or don't feel good. But other times I don't like it. I'll be playing with Karl, and she'll come in and pick him up and take him off with her. I don't like that at all.

I take Karl with me everywhere I can, and my mother is constantly telling me I shouldn't do that, that I'm not being fair to Karl. But if I had to stay home all the time with him, I'd be miserable. And if I'm miserable, so is Karl. I think it's all right. He's seeing new things, being with people. He's learning more from going places with me.

Sometimes I have to explain to my mom that I have taken on this responsibility of being a mother, and I want to do it the whole way. I know when Karl is hungry, when he needs a bath, etc., but my mom still tries to tell me to do all these things. I try not to let it bother me — but it does.

Because I'm underage, it would be hard to live alone. I wouldn't have anybody around when I'm sick.

I wouldn't have anybody to talk to — and I couldn't
afford a place of my own.

                                    Kimberly, 17 - Karl, 2 months

Role of Brothers and Sisters

If you have brothers and/or sisters living with you, you'll
need to consider their feelings, too. Will their lives change
much because of your baby? Will they be expected to do
more of the housework because you'll be so busy with
your child?

How do you think they will feel about that? There
probably is no "right" answer, but it's a topic you and your
family should consider, preferably before your baby
arrives.

Sometimes my sisters want to give me advice. I let
them say what they want. I can ignore them.

For example, just lately Stevie gets crabby when
he's having a bowel movement. When they see him
fussing, they tell me to feed him. Or they think we
should "do" something. They'll shake toys in front of
his face. But he's too little to care much about toys.

When he was just two weeks old, they wanted to
shake rattles in his face. He didn't want that. He's just
a little baby. I'd tell them that, and they'd go running
to tell my mom, "Alison doesn't want us to do any-
thing with her baby." My mom would laugh and tell
them I know what I'm doing.

I think my sisters get annoyed at my being here all
the time with the baby. But when I ask them to baby-
sit so I can go out for a little while, they usually
refuse.

                                    Alison, 18 - Stevie 2 months

Extended family — more commotion, more love.

Key — Taking Responsibility

*I thought it would be my mom taking care of
Racquelle all the time. With my two sisters who got
pregnant at 16, she took over. They didn't know
anything about taking care of their babies.*

*When I brought Racquelle home, I took care of her
by myself all the time. I showed my mom I could do it.
So now that she knows she doesn't have to take care
of her, she will babysit sometimes when I want to
go out.*

Cheryl

Sometimes young mothers have more help than they
want. If this happens to you, perhaps you can help your
family understand that all of you — your parents, siblings,
baby, and you — will be better off if you take the primary

responsibility for caring for your child. If you start out,
tired as you are, showing them that you know how to be a
good parent, they may be less likely to give you more help
and advice than you feel you need. Alison's mother
commented:

Alison does everything. If I weren't working it
would be harder not to take over. I'm surprised at
myself that I haven't done that. That was a concern I
had when she was pregnant. I knew this had to be her
baby, her responsibility. I love babies, and I like to
take care of them, but I've not gotten up even once
with Stevie. In fact, I don't hear him cry at night!

Alison added:

Stevie's such a good baby, but I do think I have to
keep him quiet. Dad can take quite a bit, but I know
he doesn't like to hear babies cry. It would be a lot
harder if he were a fussy baby. Then I think my family
might get irritated. But since he sleeps in my room, I
just pick him up and nurse him when he wakes up at
night. He goes right back to sleep.

If you're a young parent living with your parents, you
may feel you have no choice. You probably also appreciate
their help. An extended family of baby, mother, and/or
father, and grandparents at its best means more love and
TLC (Tender Loving Care) for baby — and that's great!
    Sometimes the relationship between a teen mom and her
mother even improves after the baby is born:

My relationship with my mom became a little better
because I started thinking about my kids and how I
wanted my kids to treat me. And I started thinking of
her as a friend as well as a mother. She really really

respects me in my motherhood. She asks to hold the baby, and that makes me feel good. She doesn't act like I'm just a little kid trying to raise a baby.

Kellie, 16 - Kevin, 3 months

Moving in with Partner's Family

If you move in with your partner's family (whether you're the mother or father), there may be added difficulties. No two families are alike, and those differences may demand a lot of understanding on everybody's part. Zandra talked about living with Nathan's family while she was pregnant, then moving with Nathan and their baby to her mother's home in another state. It's a difficult situation:

Before, I lived with Nathan's family when I was pregnant. Nathan was going to school, he was working . . . I would just stay in the room all day when I was there. I didn't like being around them when he was at work or at school. If Nathan wasn't there, I wouldn't eat with his family. I would take my food to my room.

But now we live here and they're 1500 miles away. And now it's hard for Nathan because he hates my family. He's a good person, he's nurturing to Dakota, but he's not happy here.

Zandra, 16 - Dakota, 11 months

Camelia worried about moving in with Jonah's family:

When I first moved in I thought everyone was against me. I thought, they're family, and they'll stick up for each other, but I was wrong.

I love my mother-in-law. She's like my second mom. Considering that I was pregnant, I was going through a lot of mood swings.

*The one thing I was mostly mad about was I didn't
have my mom here to go to. It was funny for me to
think that way because I was the one who decided
to move out.*

Camelia, 16 - Buchanan, 6 months

If you're from a different culture than your partner, it
may be harder.

*It's real hard because Colin's family are all in a
different culture. I'm white, and they're Mexican.
That makes it hard. They have different upbringing
than I have. I feel like I'm being forced to grow up the
way they grew up, and I'm not used to that.*

*Are we going to bring Clancy up to know both
English and Spanish, or just English? I would like him
to know both languages, but hopefully I would teach
him to speak Spanish only to those in the family who
speak only Spanish. There are a lot of them.*

*I'm trying to learn Spanish, but I find it real hard
to communicate with his family. When they want to
know about the baby I usually go through Colin or his
dad, who know both languages. I'm trying to learn it
so I can talk to Clancy in both languages.*

Chelsea, 19 - Clancy, 2 months

Chelsea is wise to be learning Spanish, and to want their
child to learn both languages. Communication is important,
and that's extremely hard if you don't speak the same
language.

Even if you speak the same language as your partner's
family, you may have been reared with quite different
beliefs and ways of doing things. Perhaps your father and
mother share the housework and child care, but in your
partner's family, mom does these things by herself.

> *When Lucas started working, everybody was
> getting mad because I didn't have a job. His mother
> started complaining to him because I'd go out with
> my friends with the baby. But why is it her business?
> We pay rent. But fine, I'll get a job.*
>
> *Then she would open our door and see a mess in
> our room. When Lucas got home, he'd start cleaning
> up, and she'd say, "Why do you do that? Why isn't
> she doing it?"*
>
> *The thing that upset me was that Lucas wouldn't
> defend me. I'd tell him, "If you're home before I am,
> you do it." Or he will wash our daughter's clothes.*
>
> *She gets mad and says, "Why are you washing her
> clothes and why are you folding them?"*
>
> Kelsey, 19 - Kamie, 21 months

Life is seldom easy when two families live together. If
you're a guest of your partner's family, you'll want to do
all you can to foster positive relationships. Your first task is
to communicate with your partner.

Communication doesn't mean you tell him (or her) how
bad his parents are. Rather, it's a matter of the two of you
working together to work through the problems. Whether
you're dealing with big issues or little day-to-day annoy-
ances, do all you can to find solutions so everyone wins.

Will Everyone Agree?

> *My mom is really good, and she helps me a lot. But
> on some things I disagree with her. I don't think you
> can spoil a newborn baby, and I feel strongly about
> that. I just don't feel you can spoil a newborn. She
> needs all the loving she can get.*
>
> *My mom tells me I shouldn't pick Patty up when
> she cries, but I won't let her cry very long. I tell Mom*

times change, she raised five, but I've learned some things, too.

Beth, 18 - Patty, 3 weeks

Whether you are with your family or your partner's, with more people in the house, there will be more interacting. There will be more people who may wake up when baby cries. There will be more people who resent the mess of wet diapers and other baby things around.

With more people, there will be more disagreement, too, as to whether baby needs to be picked up when she cries, or whether she is simply trying to get to sleep. "Don't pick her up, you'll spoil her" can be fighting words if it's Grandma talking to a young mother who is convinced that a newborn's crying means something is wrong.

Your best defense is education. Learn how and why things happen to baby. Your informed responses to suggestions from others are great tools.

Three generations, baby, parents, and grandparents, living in the same house or apartment means everyone must give a little, sometimes a lot. When you get uptight, try to remember that all that extra love can be a real advantage for your baby.

---

*For further reading, see **School-Age Parents: The Challenge of Three-Generation Living** by Lindsay.*

Part III
Your Baby Is Ready to Move

During the middle four months of your child's first year, she will change from a lie-where-you-put-her baby to a little person on the move. She may not be standing or crawling by her eighth-month birthday, but she's getting close. Her development during this time is described in the next chapter.

Keeping baby safe will become a greater challenge as he starts crawling. Childproofing is discussed in chapter 11.

Baby's eating habits change, too, from four to six months of breast- or bottle-feeding only to small beginnings in the solid food arena. Chapter 9 is about that first move toward the kinds of food you eat, that short period of time when your baby is ready for solids but can't yet manage lumps in his food. It's a time when you'll still do most of the feeding, although baby will eat some foods with his fingers.

Playing with baby becomes more and more fun for him and for you. Perhaps in chapter 10 you'll find some new ideas for playing with and teaching your child.

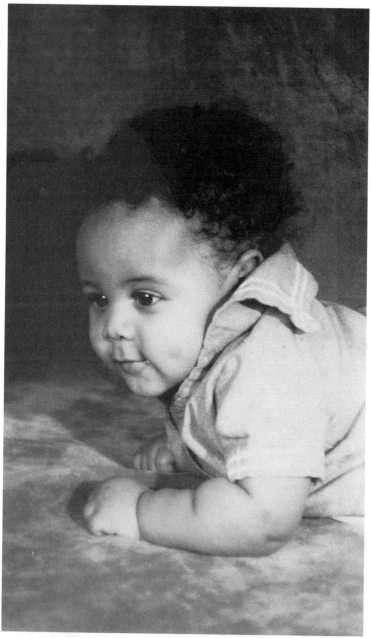

His curiosity makes him want to touch and handle everything.

8

Baby Is
Much More Active

Juan likes to feel and chew on things. He knows different textures, and if it's coarse, he doesn't like to hang on to it. He likes his little bunny and dog because they're soft.

Ginny, 17 - Juan, 4 months

Nick sits up by himself for a long time, then he collapses. Then I set him up again. When he gets tired, he lies down. He entertains himself for a longer time now.

Theresa, 16 - Nick, 6 months

Delphina has a mobile of bears with music, and she grabs them. She loves sitting in a swing and watching the mobile go around.

Shoshana, 17 - Delphina, 4 months

His Interests Grow

*Now at five months, Orlando is more alert, more a
person. When he was little, he just lay there and really
couldn't see me clearly. Now he rolls over, coos,
growls (really!), plays with his feet and his hands, and
laughs.*

*When he was a newborn I held him a lot, and he
loved that. Now, I hold him and play with him. I spend
about as much time playing with him now as I did
holding him, perhaps a little more. He's teething and
is a little fussy.*

Holly, 17 - Orlando, 5 months

By four months, your baby's curiosity is growing fast,
and he wants to touch and handle everything possible. A
simple face drawn on a paper plate and taped to his crib
interests a newborn. No longer, however, can you give him
such a flimsy thing to look at.

He will enjoy a well-designed mobile, but now his
mobile must be strong enough to be hit, pulled, and abused
— if he can reach it at all. It's less frustrating to baby to
have the mobile placed close enough to be touched and
handled.

At this age, he needs a crib toy. It must be "battable" and
safe. It also should make a noise, such as several rattles
hanging within batting range. Using string around baby is
risky in case he could wrap it around his neck. An inexpensive cradle gym is a good purchase. It should have simple
objects that baby can hit, pull, and handle.

Sometime during this stage, baby will be able to reach
for things he sees. This is quite different from his earlier
batting at objects. Now he sees the object, reaches for it
smoothly, and opens his fingers before he touches it. What
a change!

He's Moving Around

Juan pulls on the handle of the cradle gym in the playpen. He pulls it down, then lets it go. He got frustrated this morning because he tried to crawl to get what he wanted, and he just couldn't do it.

Ginny

Four-month-old Sara stays pretty much where you put her. Lay her on a blanket with a few toys. Go back ten minutes later and she's in the same general area. She may be able to dig her toes in and scoot a little. Soon she will turn from her back to her stomach and back again, but she's not moving all over the apartment yet.

Eight-month-old Sam is an entirely different being. He's sitting up. He's getting ready to crawl. In fact, lay him on a blanket on the floor, turn your back for a second, and he may be across the room! He may be crawling already.

The physical changes happening between four and eight months in a baby's life are startling. Until he's four or five months old, baby is limited to lying on his back or his stomach or being propped up by someone else. He depends completely on others to move him from place to place.

By about 61/2 months, many babies sit up by themselves. Many start creeping or crawling about a month later. But, as in every kind of development, each child is different. Don't worry if your baby isn't sitting up or crawling yet.

Wayne's been crawling since seven months, but he didn't sit up until about that time. I like the crawling because now he can do something.

Lorice Ann, 23 - Wayne, 9 months; Kelton, 7 years

Sometime toward the end of this four-to-eight-month period, your baby may pull herself to a standing position. She'll hang on for dear life to her crib railing or to the arm

of the couch. At first she's pleased, but in a minute she may
start crying. She doesn't know how to sit down again!

You can help her learn to sit down. Show her how.
Gently bend her knees as you talk to her. She'll sit down,
and two minutes later she's up again. It may take several
days for her to learn to get down by herself.

Comparing Babies

The age at which a baby sits up, crawls, and walks seems
to have nothing to do with her I.Q. when she's older.
Comparing your child's development to that of your
friend's child can be fun as long as you don't take these
differences in development as negative for either child. The
baby who doesn't move off the blanket during much of her
first year may be one of the brightest kids around.

To some parents, baby's intellectual development is very
important. There are many kinds of intelligence. One child
may be very interested in learning pre-reading skills;
another may be fascinated with insects and spend lots of
time watching them move. Perhaps your child can hardly
wait for an opportunity to help mom or dad fix things
around the house.

The child who doesn't read well in kindergarten may be
repairing the family car a few years later, a task her reading
brother may find impossible.

Remember that your child, whatever his abilities, is
important; your child is a fun person. Enjoy him. Whether
or not he is "brilliant" is not terribly important.

Curiosity Leads to Crawling

*These past couple of weeks Jonita has started
pulling herself up on the chair. She likes to stand and
doesn't like to sit very often. This morning my sister
got her up and set her in the living room. She went in*

*the bedroom, and when she came out, Jonita was
clear across the room!*

Ellen, 17 - Jonita, 6 months

As baby lies on the floor or sits in his infant seat, his
curiosity is building rapidly. Put yourself in his place.
Imagine what it must be like not to be able to move. You
see all those exciting things around you, and all you can do
is look at them. Imagine the frustration!

Wanting to satisfy his curiosity is baby's biggest reason
for learning to crawl. He likes the exercise and being able
to move his body, but satisfying his curiosity is the big
incentive.

Before they walk, babies get around in a variety of ways.
Classic crawling is getting up on his hands and knees and
moving around. Some babies pull themselves along on their
tummies. Others stand up on their feet and hands, then
"walk" like a little puppy. Whichever method your baby

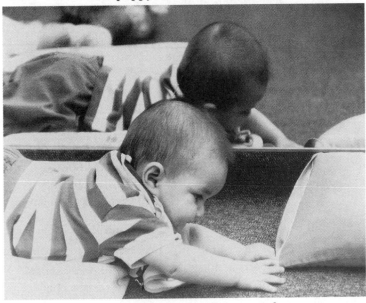

He examines everything he can reach.

chooses, he is delighted that he can finally get around.

Did you know that baby needs your help to learn to crawl? No, you don't need to show her how to move her legs and arms. It is important, though, that you give her lots of opportunity to move around. That means not caging her in a playpen or setting her in her high chair for long periods of time.

Instead, put her on the floor on a blanket. Dress her so she won't hurt her knees and let her go. And before you know it, she will go — all over the house! Of course, you need to baby-proof your home by this time.

> *When Lynn started crawling, I couldn't sit around any longer and not watch her when she was on the floor. She's going all the time — and so am I!*
>
> Sheryl Ann, 17 - Lynn, 7 months

> *Clark didn't crawl two weeks ago, but now he speeds all over the place. What a change!*
>
> Kathleen, 18 - Clark, 7 months, and Aaron, 2 years

Build Trust by Responding

> *Jay is a good baby. He only cries when he wants something, has messy pants, or wants to eat. He does have his fussy days when he just wants to cry. Yesterday was one of those.*
>
> *I barely got home from school when he started crying, and he didn't stop until 10 p.m. when he went to bed. I think he's cutting teeth. Sometimes it's hard having a baby.*
>
> Bev, 17 - Jay, 8 months

It's still important to respond to your baby's cries as promptly as possible. Letting him learn he can trust you to take care of his needs is not going to spoil him. Unhappy, dissatisfied, "spoiled" babies are far more likely to be babies who are already learning they can't depend on mother to come when they need her.

> *I've heard so many times that I'm spoiling Buchanan. I can't stand it when people tell me how to raise my son. I don't believe in spoiling him. I just want him to be secure, to know I'll be there for him. If he's crying, he's crying because he needs something. I want him to know that if he cries, I'll be there.*
>
> Camelia, 16 - Buchanan, 6 months

Continue to hold your baby and to rock him. Now you'll be able to do a lot more with him. This stage is usually delightful for parents.

Some babies have a hard time settling down to sleep. They may fuss for a time before going to sleep, and that's okay. If the fussing changes to a hard cry, of course it's time to do something.

Throughout most of this period, baby may be happy most of the time, just as he was in the less active one-to-four-month stage. He giggles and laughs, mimics what you're doing, and generally has a wonderful time throughout much of his day. But he wants you to be nearby. If mother leaves for more than a few hours, the separation may be hard on both her and her child:

> *I went to the mountains for three days without Lynn, and it was hard. I couldn't really have fun because I was always thinking about her and wondering if she was all right. I knew she was being taken care of okay, but it still bothered me. When I got back, she wouldn't let me out of her sight.*
>
> Sheryl Ann

This doesn't mean it's wrong to take some time for yourself. It does mean you will choose carefully the person who will care for your child while you're gone. You also

She loves to play on the floor with Mom.

need to be prepared for a short period of increased
dependence on you when you return.

Baby's Fears

Some babies develop rather strong fears. Sometimes it's
the vacuum cleaner. It might be the lawn mower or some
other loud noise. He may decide he wants nothing to do
with new places or different situations. A trip to the store
may upset him.

If it's the vacuum cleaner, you could try using it while he
sleeps. A better way is to let him look and explore the
vacuum cleaner before you turn it on. Then hold him with
one arm (lovingly, not scoldingly) while you clean for a
few minutes. Don't overdo it, of course, but he may accept
the noise under these conditions.

Always, whatever his age, treat your child's fears as the
realities they are. It absolutely does not matter that you

know "there is nothing to be afraid of." The fact is that he is afraid. You need to help him deal with his fear, not scold him.

Time for Teeth

When Dale was teething, I didn't even know he was. He would be cranky once in awhile, but I just thought he was tired or something.

Arlene, 17 - Dale, 11 months

The "average" baby (yours may be quite different) cuts her first teeth when she is six or seven months old. She will probably get her lower incisors first. By eight or nine months, she may have four of her upper teeth.

Some babies fuss when their teeth are cutting through their gums. Others seem to notice very little, if any, discomfort. One mother reported she knew her child had cut his teeth when she heard the spoon clanking against the tooth.

For some babies, teething is a painful experience. She may want to bite everything in sight. Give her a teething ring. Store several in the freezer. If the ring is cold, she'll like it better.

Robin has a tooth that's not all the way in. She's keeping me up for hours. Nothing seems to work. I put teething lotion on it, or ice cubes, but nothing helps.

Melinda, 15 - Robin, 9 months

Try freezing thin slices of cantaloupe for your teething baby. Of course you carefully remove all seeds and rind from the melon. Baby can suck on the frozen piece and, when it thaws, gum it and swallow it.

You can buy teething lotion which may help soothe

painful gums. Put it on baby's gums a few minutes before feeding time. It may take away some of the pain so that she can eat more comfortably.

Baby may drool while she's teething. If so, tie a terrycloth bib on her.

These first teeth are not chewing teeth. They won't help much when she's trying to chew food. She'll still have to gum solid food with lumps in it. But she may try to chew the nipple on her bottle.

If you're breastfeeding, she may try biting your nipple. If the nipple is well back in her mouth as it should be for sucking, she can't bite. The only problem is when she stops sucking and decides to play.

If she bites, remove your nipple from her mouth with a firm "No." Pause for a few seconds even if she's whimpering because you've taken her food away. Then if she wants to eat, let her. But don't let her bite you. Many breastfed babies learn not to bite after only a day or two of this approach.

If your baby gets a fever, don't blame it on teething. She may fuss, she may even have a tiny bit of fever if her teeth are bothering her. But if she has a "real" fever (higher than 101^0), she's sick. A fever indicates an infection. Call your healthcare provider.

Guard against cavities in those little teeth from the beginning. Encourage her to drink water. It's certainly better for her teeth than are sweet drinks, and water helps rinse milk and other foods out of her mouth.

Avoid sweet foods. During this period you should be able to keep candy and other sweets almost entirely away from baby. If she doesn't know about them, she won't cry for junk foods. The same suggestion applies to soda and other soft drinks. Don't even give her a taste. Her teeth will thank you.

Nursing Bottle Syndrome

Even a bottle of formula can be a problem for baby's teeth. True, her teeth need a lot of calcium in order to develop properly and to stay healthy. The best source of calcium is formula (and milk). She needs about 20 ounces of formula each day at this stage.

A bottle of formula is a problem if she keeps the bottle nipple in her mouth as she falls asleep, and it stays there. Formula dribbling into her mouth during the night keeps her teeth covered with a film of milk. Formula, nutritious as it is, has enough natural sugar in it to damage teeth if it stays there hour after hour.

Dentists see so many toddlers with rotten little teeth in front that they have given this condition a name: Nursing Bottle Syndrome.

The solution, if baby wants a bottle in bed with her, is to fill the bottle with water. Fruit juice is even worse than formula because it has more sugar in it. If she needs the sucking when she goes to sleep, she can get it with a bottle filled with water or with a pacifier.

Taking a bottle of formula to bed can become a very strong habit, a habit that is hard to change. If you hold her while she drinks her bottle at bedtime, she won't need more formula in bed. When she's big enough to take the bottle to bed with her, always put water in it. Then she won't risk having Nursing Bottle Syndrome.

Tremendous Changes Already!

Your pre-toddler has changed tremendously in these first eight months. As she sits up, possibly stands, maybe scoots across the floor, you may think she's into everything already. But amazingly soon she will be walking, then running. Keeping up with her will be — already is — an exciting challenge. *Are you ready?*

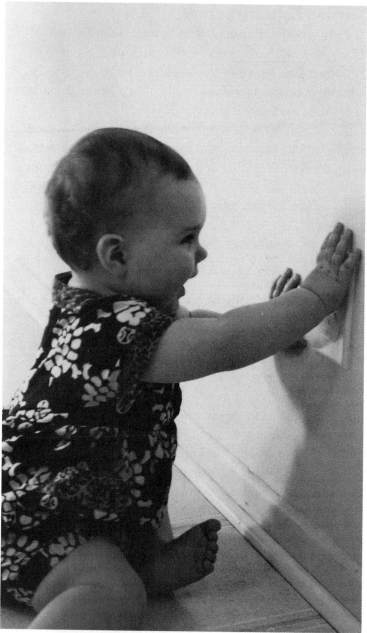

Protective covers on the electrical outlets help keep her safe.

9

Accident-Proofing Your Home

I keep a lock on the door under the sink so Gary can't get into it.
Jan, 15 - Gary, 12 months

My mother always said not to put my soaps and things in a low cupboard, so I keep them up high above the stove.
Olivia, 20 - Henry, 11 months

Leon pushes a chair up to the counter and gets up in the top cupboard looking for little goodies. I have glasses up there, so I suppose I'll have to fasten the doors shut. I keep him locked out of the bathroom.
Tamera, 21 - Leon, 10 months, and
DeeDee, 4 years

Accidents — Often Deadly

Accident-proofing your home is *absolutely* essential if you have a baby, toddler, or preschooler living there. Accidents injure and kill many young children every year. In fact, accidents are by far the greatest cause of injury and death for this age group — thousands are permanently crippled or killed annually. Keeping your child safe is one of your biggest challenges.

The chief causes of fatal accidents for children under one year are suffocating and choking. Cars, fires, drowning, and poisoning cause the most fatal accidents for toddlers and preschoolers. Falls cause about forty percent of all injuries to young children.

Warning
Never leave baby alone on a changing table, bed, or other off-the-floor surface for a second. The baby who couldn't turn over yesterday may do so today.

When you visit friends, put your tiny baby's blanket on the floor. She can nap there as well as she could on the bed, and she'll be much safer. She can't fall off the floor. Be sure she's protected from house pets and small children.

Your baby should not have a pillow in her bed. A pillow could cause a breathing problem if she got her face buried in it. If grandma made a beautifully embroidered pillow for her, appreciate it, but keep it out of her crib.

Until she can turn over by herself, always lay baby on her back to sleep. This lessens the danger of SIDS (Sudden Infant Death Syndrome).

A propped bottle is dangerous for infants. Baby could choke from her formula coming too fast from that propped bottle. She could also choke on milk curds if she should spit up. She might be unable to clear her throat.

Start with the Kitchen

Dangers multiply rapidly when your child is crawling, then walking. Accident-proofing involves far more now that he can plunge so quickly into risky situations.

The kitchen is a marvelous learning laboratory for babies and toddlers. Designing it so it's safe for your baby is an important challenge. Hazards in many kitchens include:

- Cleaning supplies (Don't keep them in the cupboard under your sink.)
- Knives
- Vegetable grater
- Ice pick
- Cooking fork
- Hot pans (Keep the handles turned toward the back of the stove.)
- Coffee pot, toaster, and other appliance cords
- Iron and ironing board (Iron when baby is asleep, then put board and iron away.)
- Gas stove with controls baby can reach

Warning

If baby gets dishwashing detergent on his fingers, he'll put them in his mouth as usual. Because dishwashing detergent is so powerful, it can burn his mouth badly. Don't let it happen!

During the years you have a baby or young child, it is terribly important that you put such dangerous items in a high cupboard. Even there, if he's a climber, you should use a secure lock.

Toddlers may turn on the hot water faucet. Be sure the water temperature is low enough not to scald baby.

When your child has a minor accident such as touching the stove and burning his fingers slightly, help him understand what happened. Don't say anything about "the bad stove" burning him, and don't fix it up with cookies. Sympathize, of course, and put ice on the burn. Also explain if he touches the stove when it's hot, he'll be burned.

Gas Stove Is Risky

If you're buying a range, you may be able to get one with controls on top at the back. If the controls are in baby's reach, you'll have to watch constantly that he doesn't turn the burner on. A gas stove without a self-lighting device is extremely dangerous in a home with little children. If it's turned on, but not lit, unburned gas will escape into the room. This could cause an explosion or asphyxiate people (cause them to stop breathing).

If you have a gas heater, have someone help you check if it has a safety valve that shuts off the gas if the pilot light goes out. If it doesn't have one and the pilot goes out, the escaping unburned gas is toxic and can cause an explosion.

The baby should not be left in a room with an unvented gas heater because the gas (burned or unburned) will stay in the room rather than going up a chimney or stack. Call your gas company if you don't know whether your heater is vented. For the same reason, you should not heat a room by leaving a gas oven door open.

If you ever smell gas in your home, check with the gas company immediately. In most areas, they will send someone out to check it at no charge to you.

Other Hazards

Sonja pulls on the tablecloth. If it were my own home, I wouldn't leave it on the table. People tell me kids have to learn not to touch it. I think when they're babies you can't do that.

Julie, 16 - Sonja, 7 months

To a creeping baby, tablecloths are to be pulled. If hot foods, even empty dishes, come down with the cloth, results can be disastrous. Even placemats can cause big problems. Our second son, when he was eleven months old, pulled on a placemat early one winter morning. Over came the cup of freshly poured coffee. His burn required emergency hospital treatment.

You know how baby loves to play peek-a-boo by putting a blanket over his face. He might do the same thing if he found a thin plastic bag. If he did, he could suffocate within minutes. The plastic would cling to his face and he wouldn't be able to breathe.

Carefully keep all plastic of this kind away from your baby. Cut up and discard such bags immediately after you get them, especially those put on the clothes at the dry cleaner's.

Even if you lock up all medicines, you may decide the bathroom is one room your baby can't enter. If she can't open doors herself, just keep the door shut at all times. Make it as safe as possible inside, however, because you know she will get in there occasionally.

During the time she is pulling herself to stand, be especially careful to keep the bathroom door closed. It's possible for a toddler to pull herself up by the edge of the toilet, lose her balance, fall in, and drown.

The day will come when your toddler goes into the bathroom herself. She may even lock the door behind her. A lock-release on the outside of the bathroom door would solve that problem. Keep the release key where you can find it quickly.

Check All Areas for Danger

I had to buy a gate to block the stairs when he first started crawling. We covered up all the sockets, and I

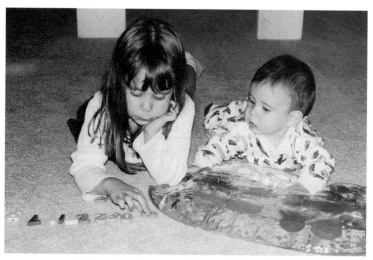

Older sister's toys can be dangerous to baby.

*shut the doors in the bathrooms because he wants to
run in there and flush the toilet over and over.*

Belia, 17 - Donovan, 2

Stairs are an obvious danger to a creeping/crawling/
toddling child. Putting a gate at the top and one at the
bottom is a solution. Put the lower gate at the second or
third step up, not at the bottom. Baby will then have a
chance to practice climbing a few steps, then coming back
down. He won't have far enough to fall to hurt himself,
especially if there's a soft rug at the bottom.

*It takes pretty constant watching where I'm living.
Quentin (Heidi's uncle) leaves little screws and things
on the floor in his bedroom. I've asked him a few
times to pick them up, but he doesn't. I get furious and
start yelling at him.*

Jenny, 18 - Heidi, 13 months

Another room you may decide to shut off, perhaps with a
gate, is where an older brother or sister plays. Satisfying

baby's curiosity there might cause more trouble with big sister than it's worth. If big sister is only a few years older, she can't be expected to understand completely what child-proofing means. Besides, big sister should not be expected to share her things, particularly not without her permission.

If you have a fireplace, open heater, heating register, or floor furnace, put guards in front of and over it. Use furniture to block off radiators.

If your toddler has learned to open doors, you can attach fasteners, the hook-and-eye kind, up too high for him to reach. You'll need some method of keeping doors closed if they lead to stairways, driveways, and some storage areas.

Your window and door screens should be securely fastened. If your house has bars on the windows, they need to be the kind that can be opened from the inside.

Sometimes I'll be doing something, curling my hair or polishing my nails. The next thing I know, Heidi has gone out the doggy door and is playing with the dogs in the back yard. I'll bring her back, and she'll do it again.

Jenny

Do you have a pet door, a little door your dog or cat can open? If it's big enough for your baby to get through, expect him to use it!

Accident-Proof Outside Areas

If you have a swimming pool, be sure it's fenced securely with a *locked* gate. Tragically, many small children die in family swimming pools each year.

If you live in an apartment complex with a pool, and you find the gate left open, report it to the manager. A toddler and a swimming pool can be a deadly combination.

A fenced-in yard is a marvelous luxury for a toddler and

her parents. If you're lucky enough to have one, enjoy it, but keep an eye on your child as she plays there.

Yards, fenced or not, and garages need to be child-proofed, too. Check for rubbish, insecticides, paint removers, and other poisons. Get rid of them or lock them up. Nails, screws, and other hardware, assorted car parts, tools, and gardening equipment should be stored out of reach or locked in the garage.

Also get rid of rusty or tippy furniture. Check hammocks, swings, and other play equipment regularly for safety.

> *One time a year or two ago Dalton fell off a lawn chair and smacked his head against the sidewalk, and he had three bumps. We rushed him to the emergency room, but he was okay.*
>
> *He was sitting there rocking himself on the chair, and I said, "If you keep that up, you'll fall." And he did.*
>
> Claire, 17 - Dalton, 33 months

You don't want to be overly protective to the point that your child is afraid to climb anything. It might be wiser, however, to calmly remove him from the tippy chair. Then explain to him why you don't want him up there. This works better than saying crossly, "If you keep that up, you'll fall."

Some plants are poisonous such as poinsettia, caster beans, and oleander. Does your yard have shrubbery or other plants dangerous to your child? Also check any house plants in your home.

Even a lovely rose garden can harm a toddler when she runs into all those thorns. Putting a temporary, but sturdy fence around your roses will protect baby. It will also protect the roses.

Is Paint Lead-Free?

Do you have furniture, walls, or woodwork in your home which were painted before 1970? If the paint contains lead, it can damage your child if he chews on the painted surface, or if the paint is peeling and he puts bits of it in his mouth. Lead poisoning can be the result, a serious problem for babies and children.

Even though more recent coats of paint in old houses are probably lead-free, chips of paint can include the bottom layers of lead-base paint. Many children eat these chips of peeling paint and plaster. Apparently they taste sweet, and children like them.

Glazed ceramic dishes imported from other countries may have lead in the glaze, lead which may contaminate food cooked or served in the dish.

If children get too much lead, they show signs of lead poisoning. "Too much" for a baby may be a very little bit of the paint. The child may become anemic and lose his appetite. He may be either listless or hyperactive and irritable. He may find it harder to learn, and may suffer convulsions and permanent brain damage from the poisoning.

If you suspect lead poisoning, check with your healthcare provider. Through a simple blood test, she can detect the condition. If lead poisoning has occurred, the doctor can recommend treatment to get rid of much of the extra lead in your child's body so he won't have the problems described above.

Car Safety

Of course you'll do everything you can to keep your toddler from running out into the street. But did you know that more children are hurt *inside* cars as passengers than are injured on the outside as pedestrians?

Traffic accidents are the leading cause of death in

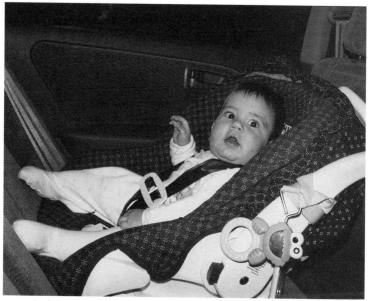

Baby must be securely buckled in when he's riding in the car.

childhood once the critical early months have passed. They
claim more lives than any disease. In addition, hundreds of
thousands of children are injured each year. Many remain
permanently disabled, physically and/or mentally.

You can protect your child from injury while riding in
your car by putting him in a safety-approved carseat (not a
car bed).

For infants, you need a seat in which the baby rides
facing backward in a semi-reclining position. It should be
held firmly in place by the car's seat belt. Children should
ride in a rear-facing carseat until they are a year old and
weigh at least twenty pounds.

When you choose a carseat for toddlers and slightly
older children, too, be sure the seat can be fastened securely
by the car's seat belt. In most states, babies and toddlers are
required by law to be fastened in a carseat when riding in
a car.

A carseat, of course, is safe only if the child is buckled in it. When your toddler decides to be negative about his carseat, it's time for you to be positive. Fasten him in it matter-of-factly, even if he's screaming. Be sure he knows you and others in the car use seat belts, too.

Safety — A Big Responsibility

You can do everything possible to safety-proof your home, but what about the dangers outside your home? Can you do anything about that? Samantha feels strongly about this issue:

Now with a child, you won't catch me partying, you won't catch me smoking. Having her changed me. Some of the girls with two kids say they're still in their gang and they're proud. You're in a gang, you're a bullet target, and so is your kid.

If somebody did something with my child, or I was at the wrong place at the wrong time, and they started shooting, I would cover my daughter. I would let them get me before they get her.

A lot of people have told me, "You should get in a gang." Why? So I can be crippled? I want to be up there running with my child, have fun with my child.

Samantha, 16 - Kaylie, 20 months

Making sure your child is safe in your home, in your car, everywhere he goes, is a big responsibility. Creating a safe environment that also allows him to explore and to learn about his world is a double challenge with double rewards.

You will find more peace of mind knowing your child is not in danger, and you will be delighted with the bright, happy individual that he is.

At six months he's ready for some solid food.

10

Baby's First Solid Food

I waited about five months to give Nick solid foods. He likes to be nursed after he eats, and then he falls asleep. I used to leak, and I wanted to nurse him, but at this point I think it's best to feed him solids first.

I give him cereal in the morning, then bring him here to the center where I nurse him.

Theresa, 16 - Nick, 6 months

I broil hamburger and put it in the blender with a little bit of formula. When we have chicken for dinner, I put it in the blender, or I give her the drumstick to chew on.

Julie, 16 - Sonja, 7 months

Don't Rush Solid Food

Your baby doesn't need solid food and generally shouldn't have it until he's at least four or five months old. Almost all babies get along best on breast milk or formula during this time.

If you feed your baby solids too soon, he is more likely:

- to develop food allergies.

- to have digestive problems.

Feeding solids to a tiny baby is usually time-consuming and often frustrating to mother and to baby. Mother spoons it in, baby rolls it right back out! Before he's four months old, baby has a well-developed sucking reflex. He sucks before he swallows his formula or breast milk. Food put in his mouth from a spoon is usually spit right back out. This is called the protrusion reflex.

By about four months of age, this protrusion reflex is gone, and he's much more able to accept food on his tongue. He can swallow it instead of letting it roll back out. It's as if he's saying during those early months, "Mom, I don't want solid food!"

In addition, if you buy strained (Stage 1) baby food, the cost can be rather high — high, at least, when you realize this is money spent which gives no benefit to baby during these early months. So why do so many parents start feeding cereal and other solids to their very young baby? They may have several reasons. First, they may think feeding him cereal in the evening will make baby sleep through the night. Research shows this is simply not true.

Sometimes people you love, perhaps your own mother, urge you to start early feeding. The research which shows that babies are better off without early solid food is fairly new. A generation or two ago, neither doctors nor the rest of us realized that early feeding can, and often does, cause allergies and stomach upsets.

When my children were babies, we thought we should start giving them cereal when they were only a few weeks old. As a result, Steve (one of my sons) has a lot of trouble with allergies. Steve and I both wish I had known to delay the solid food.

Even your doctor may tell you it's okay to start feeding solids to baby when he's very young. If this happens, talk to him. Some healthcare providers seem to think all mothers want to rush solid feeding. After discussing it, you and your doctor may agree baby doesn't need cereal yet, and that it's all right to wait until he's at least four months old.

Solids by Six Months

Ideally, then, you don't feed baby solid food for at least four months. It's important, however, that you do start spoon-feeding her and giving her finger foods by the time she's six months old. Reasons to feed solid food to baby by six months include:

- She needs nutrients she isn't getting from breast milk or formula.

- She needs to learn to eat solids, a quite different process from getting her food through sucking.

- Four to six months seems to be the ideal age to help baby learn this new method of eating. By this time it's also important that she learn to eat a variety of foods.

Rice Cereal First

Start with infant rice cereal. Use the dry, iron-enriched kind that you buy in a box. Rice is less likely to cause allergies than other kinds of cereal such as wheat. Above all, don't start with the mixed cereal. If she's allergic to just one of the ingredients, you won't know which one it is.

Eating is serious business.

Mix the dry rice cereal with a little formula. If you're breastfeeding, you can pump enough milk for her cereal at first. She'll be more willing to accept the cereal if it smells and tastes somewhat like her formula or breast milk. Mix enough liquid with the cereal to make it quite thin at first.

Carefully choose the "right" time for teaching baby to eat solid food. Don't attempt spoon-feeding at first when she's terribly hungry. She would be furious at the delay in getting the bottle or breast she wants.

She needs to be reasonably hungry or she won't bother trying this new food. About half-through her breast- or bottle-feeding is usually the best time.

A small, narrow, shallow-bowled spoon with a fairly long handle works best for these early feedings. To baby, eating from a regular teaspoon feels like eating from a huge tablespoon would feel to us. (Try it sometime. You'll see why she needs a little spoon to match her mouth size.)

If baby doesn't sit up by herself yet, put her in your lap or in her infant seat for her first solid food experience. She needs to be a little more upright than for her breast- or bottle-feeding.

Next step is for you to relax! If she doesn't like cereal the first time, that's okay. Try again tomorrow — and the next day. If she still resists, wait a few days before trying again. If she swallows a bit of cereal, congratulate her. Be thrilled. Show her you're pleased. If she doesn't eat it, don't make a big deal of it.

Warning

Sometimes parents mix cereal and formula together, then feed it to baby from a bottle. *Don't!* Your baby needs to learn to eat from a spoon. An infant feeder which practically "injects" the food into her mouth is bad, too. *Don't buy it.*

Let her drink formula and water from a bottle. Help her learn that solid foods are eaten from a spoon. Fairly soon she will also learn about finger foods.

Vegetables, Fruits for Baby

Start feeding baby vegetables, fruits, and their juices sometime between his fifth and seventh month. Traditionally, babies have eaten white fruits first, usually applesauce or pears, perhaps because almost all babies like the taste. After the sweet taste of fruit, however, baby may balk at vegetables. You may decide to start with a vegetable, perhaps squash, sweet potatoes, or carrots.

Mashed banana is often one of the first foods given to baby. Most babies like it, and it's super-easy to mash to a smooth consistency. You *don't* need to buy it in a jar!

If you decide to buy Stage 1 baby food, read the labels

carefully before you buy. Choose basic fruits, vegetables, and strained meats.

Don't buy combination meals because you get less protein per serving with them than you would if you mixed together a jar of meat and a jar of vegetables yourself.

If the label tells you the food contains a lot of sugar and modified starches, don't buy it.

Skip the baby desserts because baby doesn't need them any more than the rest of us do.

You Can Fix It Yourself

Fixing food for baby is easy. If you have a blender, use it. Or you can buy a baby food grinder for just a few dollars. With it, you prepare small amounts of food for baby. The blender is easier for fixing larger amounts, and works better during the short time baby needs very smooth, strained or Stage 1 food.

Important vitamins are lost when you cook foods in boiling water. The steam method of cooking will save more of those vitamins. The food is held above the boiling water so it will cook only in the steam.

A steam basket, available in most department stores, fits into most pans. You need to use a pan with a tight-fitting lid. Many adults prefer steamed vegetables because foods cooked this way retain more natural flavor.

If you're cooking for the whole family, be sure to take baby's portion out *before* you add salt, sugar, and other seasonings. She won't mind. A craving for extra salt is learned by eating foods with added salt. Don't season her food to meet your taste. You're fixing it for your baby, not yourself.

Too much salt in one's diet can cause numerous health problems including hypertension. Eating sugar may cause a craving for sweets, and is hard on her teeth. Help your baby avoid these problems by having as little salt and sugar as possible in her diet.

If possible, use your family's meals as a start. If you're having a vegetable, put a small amount (without seasonings) through a baby food grinder. Perhaps you're having a meat that is also suitable for blending. Do you like applesauce? If so, share it with baby.

Cook and Freeze

If your family meals aren't suitable for baby, you can still prepare her food without spending a great deal of time. Best approach is to cook and freeze ahead. See recipes on page 144.

Simply pour prepared food into ice cube trays. Freeze it quickly, keeping protein food, vegetables, and fruits separate. Then store the cubes in plastic freezer bags or in reusable containers. Be sure to label and date the food you're freezing. Use it within two months.

With a little planning, you can have a nice variety of food stored in your freezer. If you fix a different vegetable for your family each night one week, simply cook at least twice the amount you need. Prepare the extra amount for baby, then freeze. Do the same with fruits. You may find it easier than running to the store to buy jars of baby food.

When you're ready to serve the cubes, thaw in a warming dish or in an egg-poaching cup over boiling water. The little individual egg-poaching pan is a convenient size and is relatively inexpensive.

You don't need to warm the food beyond room temperature. Baby's taste buds are not fully developed, and what seems warm to you may seem hot to baby.

If you wait until he's six months old to start baby on solid food, you'll need to use blended/Stage 1 food for only a couple of months. He can be eating table food, much of it

Recipes for Baby

Cooked Fruit

- Wash, peel, and cut apples, peaches, pears, plums, or apricots into small pieces. Remove pits.
- Simmer or steam until tender (10-20 minutes). Don't add sugar.
- Using baby food grinder or blender, blend until smooth.
- You can also buy fruit canned in water or its own juices, no sugar added. Grind or blend as above.

Cooked Vegetables

- Simmer cut-up vegetables in one inch of water or steam over boiling water until tender.
- Mash or blend the vegetables.
- Add cooking water to get the right consistency.
- You can also buy vegetables canned in water without seasonings. Grind or blend as above.

Meat for Baby

- Use meat you've cooked for your family.
- Blend to a smooth consistency.
- Add a little water, broth, or juice as needed.

* Uncooked Fruit

- Wash and peel an apple, pear, peach, or apricot.
- Add a little water. Blend.
- *** NOTE: Offer after six months of age.**

mashed, by the time he's eight months old.

Even if you don't want to prepare smoothly blended baby food yourself, you surely won't buy jars of Stage 2 or Stage 3 food. Feeding him from the family meals is so little bother to you, and it's better for baby. Simply put food through a baby food grinder until he's ready to chew the real stuff.

At first, offer baby only one new food each week. If he's allergic to that food, if he gets a rash or seems to have a digestion problem, you'll know that particular food is probably causing the problem. If you fed him a new food each day, you wouldn't have any idea which one to remove.

Finger Food for Baby

Give him finger foods as early as he can handle them. By the time he's six or seven months old, he can pick up small slices of banana or Cheerios. Before long he'll be ready for graham crackers, pieces of

Finger food to study —and to eat.

toast, teething biscuits, even little bits of meat and cheese.

Plain, unsweetened Cheerios are a marvelous early food-toy. He'll pick one up in each hand, look at it, stick it in his mouth. They contain some nutrition and, most important, are very low in sugar.

Don't give him sugar cereals. Such "cereals" should be labeled breakfast candy. Some are actually more than half sugar!

Your baby can probably:

- Hold and gum a teething biscuit by five months.

- Handle little pieces of hard-boiled egg yolk (no egg white yet) by six months.

- Eat dry unsugared cereal, soft toast, French toast, cooked carrot and potato pieces, peas with skins broken, even diced liverwurst sandwiches by seven months.

He can handle all these things himself by eating with his fingers.

Drinking from a Cup

I'm trying to give Orlando a bottle occasionally, but he doesn't want one. He does good already with a cup. He holds on to it, and he can take it right to his mouth although his coordination isn't very good yet.
                                    Holly, 17 - Orlando, 5 months

When she's five or six months old, offer baby a little formula or juice in a cup. You can buy a cup with a lid and a spout as a bridge between bottle and cup. Before long, she'll be able to drink a little formula, water, and juice from her cup.

Nick is learning to drink from a cup. Yesterday I gave him a training cup, and he's learning how to use

*it. He eats flour tortillas. He eats crackers and holds
them himself.*

Theresa, 16 - Nick, 6 months

When He Feeds Himself

Learning to eat solid food is an exciting milestone for baby, and for you. As long as you don't rush the process, you both can enjoy the experience.

For two or three months, preparing his food (or perhaps buying jars of prepared Stage 1 food) is another task you do for your baby. Feeding him provides more togetherness. Keeping mealtime pleasant is important.

Sometimes he won't want that new food you're serving him . . . perhaps because he isn't hungry, or maybe he doesn't like it. This is not the time to force him to eat. In fact, insisting he eat when he doesn't want to is never a good policy (unless necessary for medical reasons).

This is the time he starts learning that a variety of foods are good. He also learns that eating can be a loving time whether he's breastfeeding, drinking from a bottle, or eating solid food.

By the time he's about eight months old, he'll be able to eat the fruits and vegetables, bread and cereals, and some of the meats you eat. Of course you'll need to mash/chop them for him for awhile yet, but he won't need completely smooth food — and you won't need to buy jars of baby food. Instead, he'll learn to eat "real" food.

*Your baby is growing rapidly — soon she'll be
a toddler!*

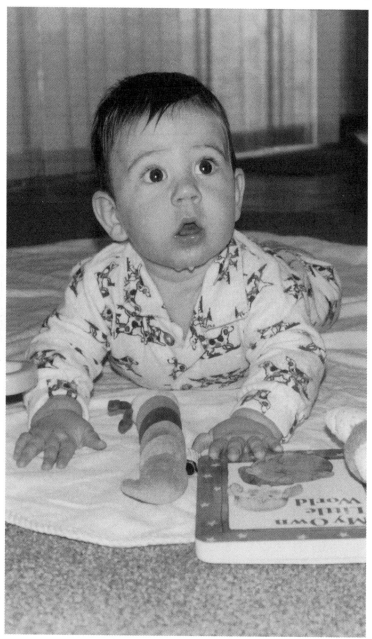

He likes playing on a blanket on the floor.

11

Playing with Your Baby

What I like about him is he's fun. He's real playful with almost everybody. You play with him just a little bit and he'll smile a lot. He always has a smile on his face. People say he looks like me.

I like taking him with me to the park when I go there with my friends to play handball. There are four or five of my friends at my house every day. They help me out a lot.

Andy 17 - Gus 5 months

I play with Orlando —clap my hands, play patty-cake, sing to him, talk to him. He holds his head up now. He doesn't like to

*play by himself yet, so I lie on the floor with him.
When he gets bored, I squeak the toys for him. He
plays with his feet when he's in the infant seat.
       He loves to chew because he's teething. He's
hanging on to things pretty well, and he chews on
everything.*

                              Holly, 17 - Orlando, 5 months

Simple Toys Are Best

*Buchanan has toys, and he enjoys playing by
himself. He has that security. I play with him some,
but I want him to be able to have his own independence, too. I've already seen that in him.*

                              Camelia, 16 - Buchanan, 6 months

Your little pre-walker may often play alone for as long as
an hour *if* mother or dad is nearby. Talk to her as you work.
Give her a different object to play with every once
in awhile.

Collect small objects for your child to play with and to
explore. Let her spend a lot of time on the floor on a blanket. In front of her, put several small items and a container
for them. Choose things that are two to five inches in size
and with a variety of shapes and textures. She'll spend a lot
of time exploring these objects and practicing simple skills
with them.

These small objects don't need to be expensive toys.
She'll undoubtedly prefer items from your kitchen drawers.
For example:

• Plastic measuring spoons and cups
• Shiny can of sardines
• Plastic freezer container
• Big pan

Put everything in the big pan, and she'll be delighted.

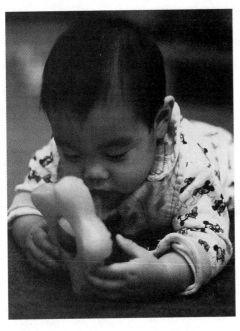

*Now he can pick something up
and carefully examine it.*

She'll look at each thing as she takes it out of the pan. She'll feel it and chew it. She may bang things together.

Be sure the items you offer her are safe. The handle on a wooden spoon or even some pan handles can be dangerous if she falls on them.

When she's tired of these things, you'll find more in your kitchen. Just be sure each thing you give her is smooth and safe for her. Nothing should be smaller than 11/2 inches. Remember, anything you give her will be mouthed if at all possible.

Nick likes a plastic bottle and other containers. I cleaned out one container and put little rocks in it, and he loves that. Of course I taped the lid on tight.
                                    Theresa, 16 - Nick, 6 months

Sometime during this stage, baby will be ready for simple stacking toys. You can give her plastic cups that will nest. Be sure they don't stick together.

Time for Games
Sonja loves to play peek-a-boo. My mom says to play it with her a lot because it's like me disappearing

*and then coming back. She'll hold covers over her
face, then drop them. I'll say "Boo!" and she'll laugh.
Or we'll play peek-a-boo around the corner.*

Julie, 16 - Sonja, 7 months

Even though baby can now play alone, give him attention when he's happily occupied as well as when he's
fussing. As he plays, talk to him, throw him a kiss, hug him
as you walk by. Smiling often at him will be easy. He'll
love to play games with you. Give him a few minutes of
your time several times a day for games.

Make a game out of baby learning to use one thing to get
another. Sit on the floor with your baby. Put a small blanket
in front of him. Put a toy on the blanket, but out of your
child's reach. Show your child how to get the toy by
pulling on the blanket. Can he do it himself?

*I put Kolbee on a blanket down on the floor, and he
tries to grab his rattles. Then it gets underneath him,
and that upsets him. I just pull it out, and then he's
happy again.*

*I make faces at him and make him laugh. I stand
him up, and he likes that.*

*I talk to Kolbee a lot. I used to say I didn't know
what to say to him, but now I just say anything. When
he sees me coming, he gets happier. He gets a kick out
of everything.*

Vanessa, 17 - Kolbee, 5 months

Specific games with baby are fun, but at this stage, they
need take only a few minutes. Patty-cake and peek-a-boo
are the old standbys.

Baby will enjoy going outdoors with you. If he isn't
crawling yet, lay him on a blanket near you while you work
in your yard.

When he starts crawling, let him play in the grass. A

little dirt won't hurt him. You need to watch him rather closely, of course.

Sunshine is lovely and provides some vitamin D for your child if his skin is exposed to it. Too much sunshine is harmful.

Babies should have very limited doses of sun. Start out with two minutes of sun a day, front and back. Don't expose baby to midday sun in the hot summer. Sunning sessions should be before 10 a.m. and after 3 p.m. Be sure to protect your baby's eyes from the sun.

If you take your baby or toddler to the beach, you'll need an umbrella unless you're staying for only a few minutes.

Walkers? Playpens?

During the early part of this stage, your child may still use her infant seat. Place her in the seat near you so she can watch you work. Be sure you set her in a safe place on the floor.

As soon as she can sit up by herself, however, she won't want to sit in it. By that time, she probably would not be safe in it, either. She might be able to tip it over.

People used to put babies in walkers, but old style (ring) walkers are not safe for baby. Also, if a baby spends a lot of time in his walker, walking on his own will be delayed. Crawling is an important foundation for walking.

Playpens are also used by many families. If you take a poll on your street, you'll probably find several babies caged in playpens. In fact, some babies put up with spending several hours a day in a playpen.

A playpen is a handy item to take to the beach. A seven-month-old baby is not ready to be turned loose in the sand. At home, the playpen can be a safe and fun place for a baby for perhaps ten minutes — long enough for you to take a shower.

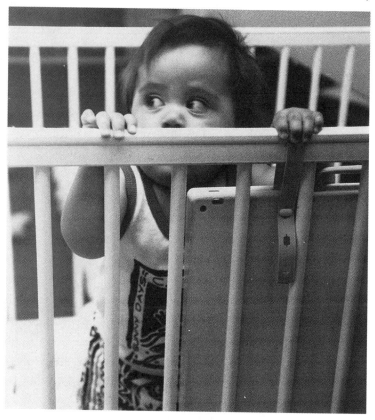

Baby won't learn much if he's stuck in a playpen.

Playpens are all right, but not for a long period of time. I would feel caged in if I had that little area. But when I'm cleaning the house, sometimes I put Sonja in there for a little while. It gets hard trying to do something now that she goes everywhere.

When she's playing in her playpen and she gets restless, I put that picture of me right outside her playpen. Sonja looks at it and gets quiet. My sister started that, and it was a great idea. Or I put a big mirror outside the playpen.

Julie

But babies generally are bored in playpens. Some scream until you let them out. Others may not fuss so much, especially if they have been stuck in their pen since they were tiny. But how much do you learn when you're bored? Not much! Your bored baby doesn't learn much either.

If you use a playpen, do so as little as possible. Your baby needs to be able to satisfy her curiosity. She will learn so much more playing with you, being near you as you work, than she possibly could learn off by herself in a playpen.

Arranging her environment so she can have freedom to explore is part of your job as a parent. Baby will appreciate your efforts. Chapter 9 offered suggestions on baby-proofing your house so you and baby can survive her creeping/ toddling months with as little frustration as possible. Making your home as accident-proof as possible is part of parenting.

She Likes Mirrors

I've held Kerry up to the mirror, and she looks and wonders what's going on. She's able to distinguish me from her. She knows who she is, but she isn't sure what to think of two mommies.

                    Leslie, 20 - Amy, 27 months; Kerry, 4 months

Babies love mirrors. Hold your baby in front of a full-length mirror and watch his reaction. He may be puzzled at seeing you there, apparently a second you. His own reflection will intrigue him because he will soon learn he can make that "person" move when he moves.

One of the best "toys" for this age is an unbreakable mirror placed six or seven inches from baby's eyes. Glass mirrors are dangerous. Look for a good quality plastic mirror four or five inches in diameter. If it isn't fairly good quality, his image will be distorted.

He Listens and "Talks"

I talk to Gary and he goos back at me. He looks at my mouth and tries to copy my expressions and what I do with my mouth.

Leica, 18 - Gary, 3 months

By two or three months, baby will hear a sound, then look to see where it's coming from. Sometime during this stage, the sound of your footsteps coming toward her room may quiet her while she watches for you. She may enjoy soothing music, although she undoubtedly prefers the sound of your voice singing to her.

Baby is becoming much more active now. It's even more important that you talk to her, but *talk* to her, don't lecture. Hold a dialog even though she doesn't answer in words. Ask questions, then pause for her answer. That's how she learns about speech patterns. Before long she'll be responding to you with her brand of talking.

Carol plays with her saliva, makes sounds by spitting it out. I heard her say Da-da once, I really did. I screamed and ran to get Mario, but she hasn't done it since.

Kristyn, 17 - Carol, 3 months

Don't use "baby talk" with her. She will learn faster if she hears words pronounced correctly. Learning baby talk is not what she needs. She wants to talk like you do.

Continue Talking to Baby

Kerry is talked to all the time. We have two other people living here, and I take her over to my mom's about three times a week. Everybody talks to her. I like talking to her because she smiles.

Leslie

Baby will begin to understand a few words during these months. He may even say "Ma-ma," "Da-da," and "Bye," but don't count on it. What you can count on is his ability to make delightful sounds. You'll hear him in his crib "talking."

When I talk with her, Sancia looks right at me and acts like she's hearing what I'm saying. She likes it when people play with her. When I change her, I look at her, and I talk with her.

One time when she was in her crib I thought she was crying. I went in, and she was lying there making little sounds, talking to herself.

Emilia, 17 - Sancia, 6 months

This is a beautiful time to put a tape recorder by his crib. Try to turn it on just before you think he'll wake up. If you walk in to see him, however, his jabbering will stop because your face and voice are even more interesting to him than the sounds he's making himself.

Your child needs you to help him develop language. You need to talk to him and read to him long before he learns to talk himself. It's especially important now to talk about the things he knows. As you change his diaper, talk about it. As you dress him, say, "Now I'm putting your shoe on your foot. Your hand goes through your sleeve." Name the parts of his body as you bathe him. Talk about the toys you're handing him.

I talk to Nick all the time. My mom talks to him, and so does my dad. He's very talkative —maybe he takes after me. We've all talked to him since he was tiny. Maybe that's why he's usually happy.

Theresa

As you carry baby around the house, show him different

objects. Name and describe such things as chair, door,
table, dish, picture, TV, couch. Take him outdoors and
name the sidewalk, tree, fence, grass. As you do this again
and again, he'll learn a lot about his world. He'll enjoy
your attention, too. Different sounds, such as music, an
airplane, a dog barking, interest him.

Sometimes when you're talking to baby, whisper in his
ear. He'll enjoy the change, and he'll learn to listen to
different levels of speech.

Reading Is Important

*I read to Buchanan and he loves it. He stares at me
like he understands what I'm saying. I know he does.*

*I think reading to him will help him form his
speech, plus it's our time together. He sits there all
quiet and listens to me. I think he likes the sound of
my voice. He looks at the book, and then he looks up
at me. He's so cute.*

Camelia

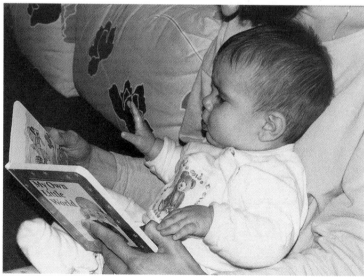

Reading with Mom or Dad is important.

If you aren't already reading to your baby, start now. Choose very simple stories, preferably with pictures of things he knows. At this age, you may have trouble getting his attention.

Reading (mostly looking at pictures) at bedtime is ideal. If baby is sleepy, he'll be more willing to sit still for a story. If he sits or lies still long enough for a story, he'll be more likely to go to bed without causing a lot of commotion.

Carlos loves his books. He'll sit there and look at the books and talk to them. I told him the story of the Three Bears and he liked it.

Renette, 16 - Carlos , 6 months

I read to Jay at night after I give him his bath. It calms him down a little.

Bev, 17 - Jay, 8 months

You don't need to buy all of baby's books. You can make them yourself. Cut big colorful pictures out of magazines. Choose pictures of things familiar to baby such as a cat, puppy, or car. Pictures of babies will fascinate him. Paste the pictures on cardboard. Punch holes in the "pages" and tie together with brightly colored yarn.

Or you may want to invest in an inexpensive photograph album, the kind with plastic over the pages. The plastic has adhesive already on it to hold the pictures in place. After you put in the pictures and relay the plastic, tape down all loose edges carefully with cellophane tape.

Again, choose pictures of subjects that are of particular interest to your child.

Self-Esteem Is Crucial

Juan plays on the floor while I do the dishes. I'll turn to him every couple of minutes and say his name,

*and I think he's beginning to know it. I don't ever call
him names like Fathead, because when he gets bigger,
he'd believe it. When he burps, I always say, "Good
boy."*

Ginny, 17 - Juan, 4 months

Self-esteem is extremely important to all of us. Parents
must think well of themselves before they can truly think
well of their baby. To feel good about someone else, you
start out by feeling good about yourself. You can help your
baby gain a good sense of self-esteem. Whenever she does
something different, learns a new skill, cheer her on. If she
bats at an object and manages to hit it, praise her. When she
can finally grab that object, get excited with her.

Calling a baby "Stupid" or some other put-down word
can too easily turn into a "self-fulfilling prophecy."

Self-fulfilling prophecy: Something that happens
because one expects it to happen.

If you tell him often enough that he's stupid, he will
decide he must indeed be stupid. If he thinks he can't learn
well, he probably won't. Of course you won't do that to
your child. Babies come equipped with a delightful urge
to learn.

Watch the baby who has just learned to turn from her
back to her stomach. She will practice her new skill over
and over and over again. She'll be thrilled each time she
does so. Being able to do something today that she couldn't
do yesterday excites her — especially if you're exited, too,
and you show her you are.

You have a wonderful challenge as you nurture your
baby's zest for life, learning, and excitement. *Enjoy!*

Part IV

Leaving
Baby Stage Behind

Sometime during the last four months of your child's first year, he will probably crawl. He may even be walking by his birthday. One thing is almost certain. He will get around at a surprisingly rapid pace.

Child-proofing your house is a big challenge at this stage. With intensive child-proofing, you make your home safe for and safe from your exploring child.

Your baby may be joining you at the table for at least some of her meals. By now she can eat many of the things you eat if you simply mash or chop the food into manageable bites. See chapter 13 for more information.

Your child continues to learn amazingly quickly. You're his teacher as you play with him, talk with him, and read to him. Chapter 14 includes more on this topic including several toys you can make.

The last chapter focuses on your future, or rather, your and your baby's future together. How do you prepare for the self-sufficient life you want? It's an important topic.

She's "cruising" now, and soon she'll be walking.

12

He's into Everything!

Gary has been walking since he was ten months old. He says "Mama," "Pa-pa." We talk to him a lot in both English and Spanish. He's curious. If he sees you doing something, he copies you. He'll come over and look. He's very close to me.

He climbs up on a board and then jumps off, but he's not on the couches yet. He loves playing outside with other kids.

He takes pans out of the cupboard and takes them outside. He picks up a lot of rocks and puts them in the pans and carries them around.

Jan, 15 - Gary, 12 months

Robin's a monster. She gets into everything. She's crawling around, pulling herself up, standing up, grabbing all sorts of things.

Melinda, 15 - Robin, 9 months

Difficult Stage for Parents

This is the busiest stage yet for both you and your child. She no longer is an infant. She's finally able to move, and move she will. Soon, in fact, she may be running.

This is a difficult stage for many parents. "She gets into everything," they say. Because she can get into so many things, people assume she should be able to understand wrong from right. She should be able to follow your orders.

This isn't true. Her memory is only beginning to develop. If she does happen to remember that you said "No" the last time she touched that fragile glass vase, she still doesn't have the self-control to leave such an inviting item alone. Slapping her hand mostly teaches her that big people hit little people. She really doesn't know why.

At this point, removing her from temptation is the smart and loving approach. You can offer her a safe toy or activity instead of the forbidden one. Chances are pretty good that she'll accept the change.

Learning Through Curiosity

Every parent has a huge responsibility to make it possible for her/his child to be as curious as possible. Curiosity doesn't thrive on a steady diet of "No" or constant imprisonment in a playpen.

Dale is curious about everything. He never stops, doesn't want anyone to pick him up. He's independent already. He has to see what everything feels like, what it looks like.

*He gets Cheerios, and loves to play with them. He
pulls the drawers open and takes clothes out. He's
trying to drink out of a cup, too.*
Arlene, 17 - Dale, 11 months

Why is he so curious? Why does he have such a tremendous need to explore? Perhaps because he spent several months lying down, then sitting, but unable to move about. As he watched his world, he became more and more curious. Now that he's crawling, he can do something about his curiosity. He can explore. And explore he will.

You'll be amazed at the extent of his curiosity. He may turn the television on and off over and over again until you can stand it no longer. Think of the power he must feel when he pushes that button and the TV comes on!

He may open and shut a kitchen cupboard door dozens of times a day. If he finds paper on the floor, he'll crumple it. He'll investigate anything and everything.

*Danette likes the wastebasket. She knocks it over
and pounds on it. She opens the cupboard doors over
and over and looks in. She'll stare, then grab
something and walk away with it.*
Caroline, 18 - Danette, 10 months

*Robin swings doors back and forth. She smacks the
bathroom door against the bathtub every morning and
wakes my brother up. She'll do that for as long as she
gets away with it.*
Melinda

You'll probably see your baby staring intently at tiny particles. As she crawls across the floor, she'll pick up that speck of dust or the crumb she dropped from her high chair earlier. During this period, you may find yourself keeping your floors cleaner than you ever dreamed possible.

Not only will your baby notice every little thing on the
floor . . . she'll also put it in her mouth. Her investigative
urge is very strong. It's your job to see that she doesn't
taste something that might hurt her.

*Jay picks up fuzz balls off the floor, string, that one
little thing is what catches his eye. He loves newspapers, loves tearing them up.*

                                                Bev, 17 - Jay, 8 months

Into-Everything Stage

*Dale climbs up on the bed and on the couch, and
he's trying to get on the table. I worry about him
because he won't stay still at all, and I'm afraid he'll
get into something. I watch him constantly.*

                                                Arlene

By the end of the first year, baby may be climbing. At
first he will struggle to get on a low footstool. Soon he will
master heights of a foot or so. If he can do that, he can
climb on a chair. From there, he can climb to the table or to
the kitchen counter. If you haven't baby-proofed your
house and your habits, you now have a problem.

*I worry about Robin all the time. She gets into
everything, and she's on the go 24 hours a day. She
falls and gets hurt because she tries to stand up on
everything. She climbs on the couch. She climbs up
me when I'm holding her in the rocking chair — she
wants to climb up and look over the back.*

                                                Melinda

Has he learned to climb stairs? Then it's time to teach
him to come down safely. Show him how to slide down on
his stomach, feet first. Even if you have a gate on the stairs,
it may be left open occasionally, and he needs to learn.

> *Alice learned how to crawl up and down stairs*
> *while we were in Texas, and she did it over and over.*
> *At first, it scared me. She went up three stairs, and I*
> *panicked and took her down. Then she started up*
> *again and fell once. From then on, she could do it.*
>   Melanie, 15 - Alice, 13 months

A one-year-old child is constantly active and constantly moving. He's always completely absorbed in what he's doing. He can be a fun companion because he is so active. He can also be completely frustrating to you for the same reason — he's so active.

Changing baby's diaper is quite a challenge during this stage. Putting a toy in his hand may distract him from his violent kicking and wriggling. You may even find you can put a diaper on baby while he's standing up.

If all of this sounds as though baby is always in command, don't you believe it! Discipline is so important from infancy on that *Discipline from Birth to Three* by Lindsay and McCullough is devoted entirely to this subject.

Of course he'll try some things that must be stopped with a "No." However, his understanding of "No," if he hears it constantly, may be "Don't try" or "Don't find out."

He won't learn as he should if he decides he isn't supposed to explore, to try new things. But he can certainly cope with the truly necessary "No."

Cruising and Walking

> *Alice isn't walking yet, but she takes a couple of*
> *steps. She holds on to the couch and reaches, then*
> *goes from the couch to the table. She's been doing this*
> *since she was about nine months old.*
>   Melanie

Soon after baby learns to stand, she may start cruising.

To cruise, she walks around while carefully supporting herself by placing her hands on the couch, a chair, or some other object.

A few babies go from crawling directly to walking. But most cruise, sometimes for several weeks, even months. At first she's extremely cautious, but before long she skims along hand-over-hand the entire length of the couch.

She'd love to have you arrange your living room furniture so she can cruise all around the room. Set the furniture close enough together to allow her to reach from one to the other.

> *Danette is walking. At about eight months, she started walking around or to the furniture. She took her first steps three or four weeks later. For a couple of weeks, she just took a few steps; then she started walking all over the place.*
>
> Caroline

Walking at nine months is unusual. The average age to start walking is between twelve and fourteen months. Some children wait a couple of months longer.

First Physics Lesson

> *Robin drops something from her high chair, watches it drop, then screams for me to pick it up. Then I tie it on a string so she doesn't hear it hit the floor. Now she's learning to pick it up with the string.*
>
> Melinda

Along about this time, while she's sitting in her high chair, baby will have her first physics lesson. She'll drop a spoon or a toy to the floor, then lean over to see what happened to it. This is serious learning on her part, and she'll try it again and again.

She can drop it, but she needs Mom or Dad to pick it up for her.

Of course mother or dad is supposed to hand the item back to her. Parents vary as to how long they're willing to continue this game. Most, however, will go along with it for awhile, especially when they realize it's a learning time for baby. You can tie some toys to the high chair with a *short* (12 inches or less) heavy string. Baby will learn to pull it back up herself. At first she won't be able to do that. She needs you to do it for her.

Supervision Needed Constantly

I worry about Maelynn getting hurt, but I try not to be overprotective. I worry about her falling down, but when she falls, I say, "Oh, oh, you fell." I don't make a big scene out of it.

I have an aunt who says, "Oh, did you get hurt? Oh no!" and this scares her kids more. I try to stay real calm so Maelynn won't get scared. I've watched my cousins. After they fall, they keep playing until their mother screams, then they start crying. I'm learning a lot from them, and I don't want Maelynn to be like them.

Joleen, 17 - Maelynn, 9 months

Your toddler requires even more constant supervision than she did when she was crawling. She will run outside to explore. By herself, she would run into a busy street. What can you do about this? *Supervise her!*

Try to be tolerant. Remember how curious she is and how impossible it is for her to control her own actions at this age.

Your baby continues to like water play. Now that she's older, this can be a problem if there is a pool nearby. A child can drown in a couple of inches of water. *Always* be with her when she's playing in water, whether it's in a tiny pool or a big one, or even in a bathtub or a pail of water.

Keeping Baby Clean ... Enough

Trying to keep an exploring toddler soap-and-water clean at all times can upset her. It may also turn her into a child who is afraid of getting dirty, which limits drastically the amount of exploring she can do.

Buy or make the toughest and simplest clothes possible for your little toddler. Make sure she doesn't feel guilty if she gets herself and her clothes dirty. This is not a stay-clean stage!

It's important, though, that you protect your child from an overdose of harmful bacteria (germs).

While there are bacteria everywhere, most of them are harmless. The body can cope with them. The body can also cope with a few "bad" bacteria. But if these bad ones have a good breeding place, they multiply rapidly. That's dangerous for baby. Good breeding grounds are food and feces.

Cooked food must be kept covered and cold or hot, never warm. If a tiny bite of cream pie falls under the table and you miss it when you clean, bacteria will start multiplying. If baby picks that tiny piece of pie up several hours later and stuffs it in her mouth, it may make her very sick.

Be extra careful about cleanliness in the bathroom, too. Be sure you always wash your hands after you change her diaper. Wash her hands for her if she explores her own body while you change her. Mop up toilet accidents and burped-up milk quickly.

Always clean up pet feces immediately. This may mean inspecting your yard every morning, even several times a day, if your toddler plays there. Children can get pin worms and other diseases from handling pet feces.

Stranger Anxiety

Maelynn likes to play with people she knows, but she's afraid of other people. She'll smile at them, but when they come up to get her, she'll hug me and not let them pick her up. You can see she's afraid, but she won't cry if she knows I'm there. I explain to her, and she seems to understand.

Joleen

He still loves people — for awhile. But by about eight months of age, your friendly baby may suddenly refuse to look at strangers. Perhaps he won't even go to grandma. Has he turned into a frightened, timid child?

Not really. But he has matured enough to know exactly whom he trusts. He generally trusts the people he lives with and who take care of him most of the time. Now he doubts the others. Sometimes this is labeled "stranger anxiety."

Give baby time. If he hides his head in your shoulder as grandma holds out her arms to him, tell her he needs a few minutes to adjust. He'll go to her under his own terms.

Dependent on Mother

I leave the room and Robin follows me because she's so nosy. She wants to know where I'm going.

*She'll follow me into the bathroom and stand and beat
on the tub. You say "No" to her, and she'll give you a
real dirty look, then cry.*

*If somebody does something she doesn't like, she
will crawl over to me and want me to pick her up. She
doesn't just cry, she screams.*

Melinda

Toward the end of her first year, she may seem very
dependent on mother. She can't bear to see you leave. She
follows you all day long.

When you take her to visit a friend, she may spend the
entire time in your arms. Only babies with good attachment
to their mothers act this way. It's entirely normal, and if she
needs you, she needs you.

This clinging-to-mother stage makes it hard to leave baby. It's not a good idea to leave while she's sleeping. When she wakes up to find a babysitter instead of mother, she may be very unhappy and frightened. It's far better to hire the sitter to come to your home a half-hour before you leave. Then baby has a better chance to adjust to the situation. If she does cry as you leave,

She sticks close to Mom.

your sitter may report that she started playing happily by the time your car was out of sight.

Playing peek-a-boo with baby from early infancy may help her realize that if you go away, you come back. It takes time to understand the important idea that, if they leave, mother and dad really do come back.

Toilet-Teaching? Not Yet!

Toilet-training, really *teaching,* has not been mentioned in these chapters because most children aren't ready to use the toilet by themselves until they're past two years old. Some aren't ready until they're three.

Trying to toilet-teach a child before s/he's ready will most likely end in a lot of frustration for both of you. Unsuccessful toilet-teaching efforts, in fact, are probably one of the biggest problems leading to child abuse.

Don't be in a hurry. Wait until your child lets you know s/he is ready. See *Discipline from Birth to Three* for an in-depth discussion of this subject.

Less Sleep Needed Now

Danette used to go to bed at 7 o'clock, but lately she's started going at 8:00. I give her supper. She plays for quite awhile, then at 8 o'clock I give her a bottle. After she drinks her bottle, she kisses me good night, and I put her to bed.

She's very very good about sleeping. She'll go to bed at 8:00, wake up next morning at 6:30. She has a bottle, then plays until 8:00 or 8:30. Then she wants her breakfast.

A couple of months ago she started fussing at bedtime. I wanted her to go to bed at a certain time, so I would put her in her crib. She would cry, but I would leave her in her crib for perhaps ten minutes.

*That seemed like a long time, but she would get tired
and go to sleep. After two or three nights, she started
going to sleep right away.*

Caroline

Your child needs less sleep as he grows older. By his
first birthday, he'll probably need only one nap per day.
Some babies want to nap in the morning. Then they get
fussy by mid-afternoon. If you put him down for a second
nap, he's awake later and later in the evening.

If you would like to have him in bed at a "decent" hour
at night, try keeping him awake a little longer in the morning. Then feed him a light lunch, perhaps at 10:30 a.m.,
before his nap. When he wakes two hours or so later, give
him another light lunch. He may last until early supper,
then go to bed for the night.

The morning nap can gradually be pushed to a later time.
Before long, he may be able to wait until noon for lunch,
then have his nap. This is important to a lot of parents.
Much as they love him, they like having their evenings free
of the constant child care they experience all day long.

Bedtime Routine Is Important

Many active toddlers are not "very very good about
sleeping." Probably at least half put up some fuss about
going to bed, especially if other family members are
still up.

Many parents prefer to have their small children in bed
two or three hours before they go to sleep themselves. Most
often a time between 6 p.m. and 8 p.m. is chosen. However,
a different schedule may work better for some parents.

Most important is that the child have a regular bedtime.
You can't keep her up until 10:00 tonight, then expect her
to lie down and go to sleep at 8 o'clock tomorrow night.

Following the same routine every night helps most children accept bedtime.

Unless bathtime is a boisterous play session, bathing her before she goes to bed may relax her.

Does your baby have a favorite blanket or stuffed animal? Encourage her to take one special thing to bed with her. Most babies have a security blanket or other object that is important to them. Perhaps it's a loved teddy bear.

Attachment to the security object may begin in this eight-to-twelve month stage, although it will become much stronger later. Many mothers report that it's almost impossible to get that special blanket away from the child long enough to put it through the washing machine.

Help her find the blanket or teddy bear that is part of the going-to-bed ritual. Read her a story. Then breastfeed her or give her that last bottle of formula as you rock and sing or croon to her. It may take half an hour for her to unwind, to relax enough to go to sleep.

If she insists on taking her bottle to bed, remember the problem caused by formula dripping on her teeth all night. The milk film can cause serious tooth decay. If she insists on a bottle, you insist on putting water in it, not formula.

If you follow the same routine with your child every night, you may find she goes to bed fairly happily most of the time. Your evenings will be more pleasant, too, if putting your child to bed is not a struggle.

Soon your baby will celebrate her first birthday. No longer is she a tiny baby totally dependent on you for moving from room to room. She's awake and she's extremely active much of the time. She's a busy little person.

Independent as she may appear at times, she still wants you nearby. You two have a good thing going as her attachment to you and love for you continues.

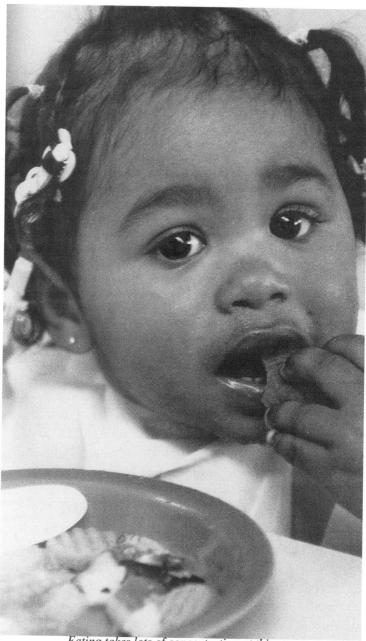

Eating takes lots of concentration at this stage.

13

Time for Table Food

Alice won't eat out of a spoon. She refuses. She'll pick it up and eat it with her fingers. She doesn't eat a lot because I guess she's attached to the milk.

First I fed her fruits, bananas, and applesauce. Then at eight months she went to real food. String beans are her favorite.

She eats any kind of meat herself, turkey, chicken, anything. She has ten teeth. She can chew the bone from the chicken wing without my cutting off the meat.

Melanie, 15 - Alice 13 months

Dale is on table food. He doesn't much like eating meat, but

he likes vegetables. I don't have to mash them. If I do,
he gets mad because he can't pick them up. He gets
mad if I try to feed him, too, so I just put food on
his tray.

Arlene, 17 - Dale, 11 months

Big Changes in Eating

I've been nursing her, and I didn't start her on
solid food until she was six months old. I don't like
giving her stuff from cans, so I boil pears. I mash
bananas for her. She eats a lot of the things we
eat now.

Zandra, 16 - Dakota, 11 months

For the first four or five months of your baby's life,
eating meant breast or bottle. Babies do better without
added food during these early months.

By five or six months, she's ready for tiny amounts of
nearly liquid rice cereal and strained fruits and vegetables.
Most of her nutrition during this stage still comes from
breast milk or formula. Those early solid foods are important mostly because she needs to learn to eat solids. Soon
she'll need more than formula, and she needs time to learn
this new method of eating.

From eight to twelve months, her eating pattern continues to change. No longer does she need her food blended
with no lumps. Whether or not she has teeth, she can gum
food after you've mashed it or it's gone through the baby
food grinder.

Most babies need strictly smooth food, whether from a
jar or food you prepare, only until they're about eight
months old. By eight months you can chop and mash table
foods for baby. Of course baby's meals need to follow the
Food Guide Pyramid just as yours do. Baby needs fruits
and vegetables, whole grains, dairy foods and protein. Fats

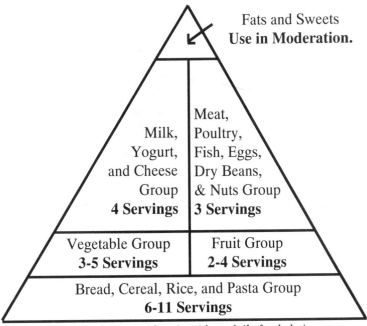

Food Guide Pyramid — A guide to daily food choices.

and sweets should be limited for baby — and for us.

When you eat out, you might take a jar of Stage 2 or 3 fruits or vegetables for baby. Adding that to the hamburger and bun he'll be eating with you, plus formula, will give him a balanced meal. Instead of the jar of baby food, you could take frozen "ice cubes" of his food from the freezer. (See page 144.) By the time you get to McDonalds, his special food will be thawed and ready to eat.

Is your baby taking vitamins? Even if you're breast-feeding, the doctor may prescribe vitamins by the time baby is a few months old.

It's important to keep mealtime pleasant. When baby refuses a food, don't push. Just offer it again in a couple of weeks. This is the time to help baby learn to enjoy a variety of foods. As his taste buds develop, he may relish something today that he couldn't stand last month.

She prefers to feed herself.

Amelia doesn't eat baby food any more. I nursed her for a long time without baby food, and people would say, "Oh, you should give her solid food."

I started rice cereal at about four months, but she didn't much like being fed like that. She has two teeth now, but she can chew anything. She can pretty much eat whatever she wants. I don't give her nuts, and she doesn't do well with strawberries — her cheeks get fiery red. I'm told they're a highly allergic food.

I don't buy baby food. I never fed her jarred meat. I think it's disgusting. I cut up chicken, steak, whatever we're eating. I cut it up good.

She loves yogurt and cottage cheese. Last night she ate a whole stick of string cheese. She drinks formula from a spouted cup.

I try to make it a balanced meal with fruit or vegetable, a grain, a protein.

Aimee, 17 - Amelia, 10 months

By the time he's eight months old, you'll be able to mash his food into small pieces. If you're serving chicken, get rid of the bone and cartilage. Then cut the meat into very small pieces for him.

Fish is excellent because it just falls apart. Of course, you have to be very careful to get all the bones out first.

> ## Warning
> Orange juice is not recommended until baby is about a year old. Some babies are allergic to it.

Many babies like cottage cheese. Just mash it with a fork.

Plain unflavored yogurt is good for baby. Don't choose the heavily sugared kind. Many children prefer the tart flavor of plain yogurt.

The above foods, along with formula or breast milk, can supply most of baby's vitamin and mineral needs. Iron fortified cereal can satisfy her need for iron. Fruits and vegetables, of course, are good sources of vitamins A and C.

Helping him learn to eat solid food is important. It's also very important that he continue getting plenty of breast milk or formula. He needs about twenty ounces each day now. Of course you don't know exactly how much he's getting from your breast, but if you're nursing him four times a day, and he seems satisfied and continues to be healthy and active, he's probably getting plenty.

Breastfeeding with Teeth?

Before Amelia had teeth, she turned her head all the way around once while she was nursing. I looked shocked and said, "No, Amelia, no. That hurts," and she didn't do it again.

Aimee

If you're breastfeeding, you may worry that when your baby has teeth, he'll bite you. Some people choose to switch to bottles at this point, but generally it won't be a problem. If baby bites your nipple, you'll respond, of course. As mentioned on page 124, if you say "No" *very* firmly and remove your nipple from his mouth for a couple of seconds, he's likely not to bite you again. Children at this age love this close breastfeeding time with mother.

Have you seen children who, at the age of one year or older, carried a bottle around with them? If you're bottle-feeding your child, and you'd rather not make weaning a hassle later, continue to hold him while he drinks his bottle. He'll get the loving closeness that breastfed babies cherish, and he'll not see his bottle as something that goes every-where with him — just as the breastfed baby can't have a breast to carry as he runs around.

Weaning to a Cup

If you're still breastfeeding her, you may decide to wean her directly to a cup in the next three or four months. If you haven't used bottles much, weaning will probably be easier for you if you let her go from your breast to the cup. Some babies are ready to drink enough milk from a cup by their first birthday. Others need to breastfeed a little longer.

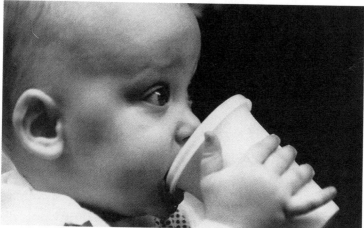

Holding his own cup is an exciting development.

If she's bottle-fed, she still needs to learn to drink from a cup. She'll spill it, even try pouring it out, if you give her too much. With patience, she'll learn. Remember, she needs about twenty ounces of breast milk or formula daily, whether by cup, breast, and/or bottle.

A spouted "training" cup provides a bridge from sucking milk to learning to drink from a regular cup. It's also harder to spill or dump formula from a training cup.

Incidentally, babies should not be given regular milk until they're a year old. Skim or low-fat milk is not good for children under two years.

When He Feeds Himself

He's trying hard to use the spoon —doesn't quite have it yet. He puts his food on his spoon, but has trouble getting it to his mouth.

Arlene

When she's eating, she likes to get the spoon and bang it for awhile, then eat for awhile, then bang it again. She doesn't like me to feed her unless she's in a good mood. She likes to feed herself. She drinks by herself from a training cup, but she still takes a bottle.

Joleen, 17 - Maelynn, 9 months

If baby wants to help feed himself, let him. He won't be able to get much food to his mouth at first. He can put his hand on yours as you hold the spoon. Or he can have his own spoon while you get most of the food to his mouth with yours.

No Junk Food Here

Dalton's teeth are decayed now because we al- lowed him too much candy and pop, and he took the bottle for too long. He took it to bed with him. The

*milk stays on the teeth, and the sugar eats away at
them. If he woke up in the middle of the night, I'd pop
a bottle in his mouth, and we'd go back to sleep while
he sucked on his bottle.*

*I love soda, and any time I had some, he wanted it.
I didn't want to hear him scream, so I'd share it. Now
we don't have soda or candy in the house. It's not fair
to eat it in front of him. Trips to the dentist are no fun.*

Clair, 17 - Dalton, 33 months

Sometimes people try to pacify a child with a sweet treat
when a hug would work just as well. In fact, hugs are
always better than junk food. Jello water and other sweetened drinks are in the empty calorie category, too. Babies
and toddlers need formula or breast milk, water and unsweetened fruit juices to drink, *and seldom anything else.*

Coffee, tea, and cola drinks contain caffeine which is a
drug. Your baby doesn't need drugs.

You'll do him a real favor if you delay giving him junk
food — soda, candy, chips, etc. — as long as possible.
Your job is to help him learn to enjoy eating the foods he
needs to grow into a healthy, capable adult.

Not the First Year

Raw, crisp fruits and vegetables aren't good for
baby until past the first year because he might choke
on them. Until he's two, in fact, if you want him to
have raw carrots, you should grate them.

Corn is not for infants or toddlers. It goes right
through in the BM without changing color or shape.

Now is the time to help your baby grow into a pattern of
healthy eating that will continue throughout his life. Feeding him a variety of foods gives him an opportunity to
develop a taste for different foods.

He's Messy!

Gilbert likes to feed himself, and he makes the biggest mess. He eats mashed potatoes and string beans. He has six teeth, and he can even chew on meat already.

Gaye, 15 - Gilbert, 7 months

A baby learning to feed himself is at his messiest. Don't be shocked. Expect it and be prepared to cope with it.

Remember how much baby likes to explore, to touch, to feel? That's exactly what he will do with his food. Some of it will go in his mouth, but at first more seems to end up on his face, in his hair, any place but where you'd like it to go. He will be delighted with the whole mess. When he wants to help, give him bits of toast or banana to hold while you feed him. He may get some food to his mouth by smearing it there with his palm.

The easiest way to feed him is to put him in a sturdy high chair. When he starts feeding himself, lay newspapers under the chair. A piece of heavy plastic protecting your floor might look better than newspaper, but you don't want something you have to clean. After each meal, just bundle up the newspapers and throw them out.

Food Is to Be Enjoyed

Looking at, handling, tasting and smelling food is part of the same exploring that begins earlier with inedibles. If he's allowed to work out his own eating habits, he learns the world is not a restrictive forbidding place where showing his own feelings and wants only brings trouble.

Keep cool and go along with his sheer enjoyment of the whole eating process. This is the best route to making his mealtimes the pleasant events you want them to be.

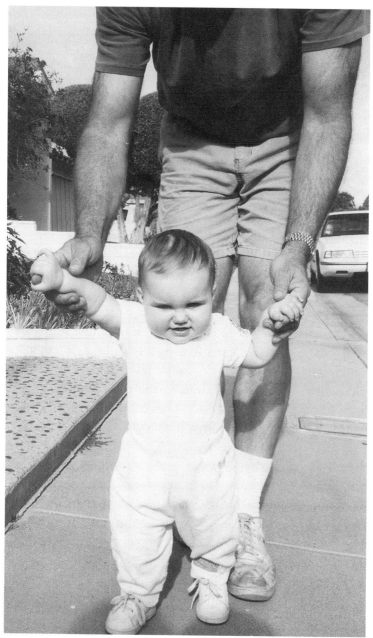

"Walking" with Dad is her favorite pastime.

14

Enjoying / Teaching Your Child

I'm enjoying Danette more as the months go by — she gets better and better! I go crazy with her new toys. We sit on the rug and play all kinds of games. I bounce her up and down on the bed.

Danette likes music. She likes to sing. I hold her and dance with her a lot. I'm crazy with her.

We go outside and I chase her all over. Jim and I take her hands and run with her.

I'll fill a can or a box with a bunch of stuff. She likes to take one thing out at a time, play with it for awhile, then take something else out and play with it.

Caroline, 18 - Danette, 10 months

A Great Time for Learning

As your child moves about, playing with him can be
even more fun for both of you. Not only is it fun, it's good
for his brain to interact a lot with you and other caregivers.
From recent brain research, we know that a child learns
many things very quickly in his early months and years. We
also know that a child who doesn't have a chance to learn
as he should during this stage may never catch up on that
missed learning.

If no one talks much to a child, if his parent is cold and
distant, the child won't learn as well as the child who
interacts with loving parents and other caregivers during
much of his waking time. The more you talk with your
child, sing to/with him, read to him, cheer him on, the
brighter he'll be.

You can interact a lot with your child even as you do
other things. By this age, she probably doesn't want you
out of her sight. Does she protest if you go to the bathroom
without her? Remember, at this stage, when you vanish, she
feels deserted.

Parents who are okay with their child constantly following them around have a wonderful teaching opportunity. If
she's nearby as you work, you can talk to her. Tell her what
you're cooking. Let her help you dust the table.

You're her first and most important teacher, and you're
working far more than a 40-hour week with her. The sheer
magnitude of her learning at this point is mind-boggling.

Bronwyn lives with her mother, but she spends a lot of
time at her dad's house. Time with Dad is more learning
time for Bronwyn:

*I take her on walks with the stroller. I sit in the
backyard and we play with my dog.*
I have a bucket full of toys, and I let her pick out

*the one she wants. If she hands me a toy, I sit and play
with her. We talk a lot. She doesn't really talk yet, but I
know she understands a lot. She's pretty amazing.*

Brady, 17 - Bronwyn, 10 months

Most children this age love to play outdoors. If you don't
have a grassy yard, is there a park nearby? Of course, being
outside when you're not quite one year old means lots of
supervision from mother, dad, or another caregiver.

*Dale loves being outside, and he likes the park a
lot. We go every Sunday because his father plays
baseball. We're constantly chasing after him.*

Arlene, 17 - Dale, 11 months

Playing Together

Your child will love playing with you. Because she likes
to imitate, she may enjoy playing follow-the-leader. Keep it
simple at first. Clap your hands, put a hat on your head, and
wave your arms.

Sounds interest your toddler, just as they have since she
was an infant. Wind chimes outside her bedroom window
are pleasant for her. Records, radio, music boxes, and bells
will intrigue her. "Singing" with you is great fun.

Dance with baby. Before she's standing or walking,
she'll love dancing in your arms. Later she'll entertain you
by dancing by herself.

Let her make her own "music" with a drum made from
an empty oatmeal box. Tape the lid on the box, then give
her a wooden spoon to use as a drum stick. Show her how
to play her drum.

Early in this stage, baby will love to pull a toy on a
string. When she's crawling, sometimes she'll go backward
so she can watch the toy as she pulls the string. If the toy
makes a noise as she pulls it, so much the better.

A favorite activity is emptying things. Your toddler will empty dresser drawers, kitchen cupboards, bookshelves, trash cans, whatever she can reach. As soon as you put things back, she'll be ready to take them out again.

I try to keep Dale out of cupboards. I put rubber bands on them. He pulls the drawers right out and takes clothes out. I tell him "No" and set him down, but he goes right back and does it again.

Arlene

Giving her a dresser drawer, a kitchen cupboard, and a bookshelf that are "hers" may help. Don't expect her to be satisfied only with emptying her toys, however. She'll like that kitchen cupboard a lot more if she can empty it of your pans and plastic containers. Of course you'll be sure all cleaning materials have been safely put away.

Amelia can get in the pots and pans in the kitchen and it's no big deal. I put them away when she's through. Some cupboards need to be locked, but I think kids should have at least the bottom drawer with things they can play with. Locking everything up wouldn't teach her anything.

Aimee, 17 - Amelia, 10 months

It may also help to give her a variety of containers to empty. Perhaps her toys can be kept in small boxes or baskets. Giving her many opportunities to empty things "legally" should help her learn not to empty and re-empty everything else in the house.

Choosing Toys

Maelynn likes to play with her beach ball and a little tennis ball. She throws it, then wants someone to bring it back again.

Joleen, 17 - Maelynn, 9 months

Balls are the best toy of all for baby. He can roll them and throw them. Once he can crawl, he can go after the ball. Soon he'll enjoy a big beach ball as well as having a wonderful time with the smaller ones. Of course he likes it best if you play with him.

One-year-olds like giant snap-lock rings and beads. They're also ready for big wooden or plastic blocks. They play with them mostly by putting them in and dumping them out of containers. Your toddler may be able to balance one block on top of another soon.

Check your child's stuffed toys to be sure the eyes and ears are firmly attached. Does the animal have a bell around its neck or even a ribbon on which baby could choke? You need to take off any part of that toy that he could pull off.

A round cereal box makes a fine tunnel. Take the bottom off, then show baby how to push a car through his tunnel. He'll watch for his car at the other end. Or you can tie a string to the car, put the string through the tunnel, and let him pull the car through.

You can also make a cardboard hill for his car. Fold the cardboard to set at a slant on the floor. Then show baby how to put the car at the top of the hill and let it roll down.

Let Him Help

Trying to copy what you do is important to a toddler. At eight months, he explores everything for the joy of exploring. Almost everything is new to him. A few months later, he wants to follow adults' examples. Earlier he banged with a spoon; now he will stir with it like mom does.

Baby loves to do what you do. Let him "help" you as much as possible as you do your work. While you're cooking, set him in his high chair near you. Are you baking a pie or making tortillas? Give him a little piece of dough

Let her "help" you as much as possible as you work.

so he can work along with you. If you're stirring something, give him a small pan and a spoon so he, too, can stir.

Interacting with Others

Busy as she is, your toddler will often show her affection
for you and for others. Toward the end of her first year, she
probably will like being around other children. She may
play by herself, but she'll enjoy watching the others.
Sometimes she may try to join their fun.

Don't expect a toddler to share her toys with another
child for a long time yet. She's still too busy learning about
herself and her world to be able to understand why Johnnie,
just because he's a guest, should play with her ball.

Do you have an older child? If he's considerably older
than the baby, he probably spends most of the time playing
with children his age. When he does interact with the baby,

he's probably quite gentle, and usually treats the baby like the baby she is.

A brother or sister not yet that mature, however, may show resentment and dislike for the baby. This stage is particularly difficult because the baby will constantly get into her brother's or sister's toys. She'll generally be a nuisance to your older toddler. The closer together the children are in age, the more hostile your older child may be.

As you supervise the two, remember that the older child, if he's under three, needs you almost as much as does the little one. You'll wonder at times how you can stretch your caring and your attention far enough for both.

Fusses between two toddlers are normal. A one-year-old and a two-year-old can't be expected to get along beautifully all the time, or even much of the time

More Language Development

Dale gets into everything. He's starting to talk, to say words. The other night I said "Good night," and he said "Night!" That's exciting.

Arlene

If you have talked to baby ever since he was born, and you've given him lots of learning experiences, he'll be working hard learning to talk by the end of his first year. He won't be saying many words yet, but he'll try.

Researchers studied a group of mothers who read to their babies 15 to 20 minutes each day. They read from simple, inexpensive children's books, pointed at the pictures, and talked about them. They used the books as the basis for talking with their infants.

Language development of these children was compared with a carefully matched group of children who weren't in the study and whose mothers did not read to them consistently. By the time they were 17 months old, the children

whose mothers had read to them had better speaking
abilities than did the other group of children.

*I read to Danette, especially Dr. Suess. I think
reading to her gives her a head start in her education.
I enjoy sitting and reading with her. I read mostly
at night, but a lot of times in the afternoon, too, we'll
read a book. Often I sit in my rocking chair, she sits
on my lap, and we read.*

Caroline

Playtime

Hide-and-seek can change. He may hide behind a chair
and ask you to find him. He'll go into gales of giggling as
you look behind each chair until you "find" the right one.

*Maelynn likes to play choo-choo. She does it
herself sometimes. She'll go behind something, then
look out at me to surprise me, and I'll laugh.*

*She was trying to make me laugh the other day. She
bumped her head lightly on the padded headboard.
She didn't get hurt, and I laughed. So she did it again
to make me laugh again.*

Joleen, 17 - Maelynn, 9 months

Get on his level. Play on the floor with him when he
learns to crawl. He'll love having you chase him all around
the living room floor. Soon he may decide to chase you
instead.

A small metal pan with a lid is a great toy, providing the
lid has a rounded edge and isn't sharp. It takes patience and
skill for baby to fit the lid on the pan. If you put a small
object inside for a surprise, he'll be even more interested.
After he has carefully examined the pan, you may need to
show him how to take the lid off and put it back on.

You can also show him how a block sounds when you

hit the pan with it. Show him the different sounds it makes when you tap his shoe with the block, then the floor. Noise is an important part of baby's life.

Water Play

Babies love water play. It can be relaxing for them, too. If you can't put baby outside with some water, perhaps you can arrange it in your kitchen without too much trouble.

First, put down a good padding of newspapers, then spread an old sheet over them. Put some water in a plastic dish. One or two inches of water is enough. You want him to splash, not flood the place. For added interest, you could add food coloring or a little baby shampoo to the water.

For all water play, an *adult* must be present at all times.

You'll find he first splashes the water, tastes it, and has a good time finding out all he can about it. You can add to his fun by giving him a couple of ice cubes. Take them out

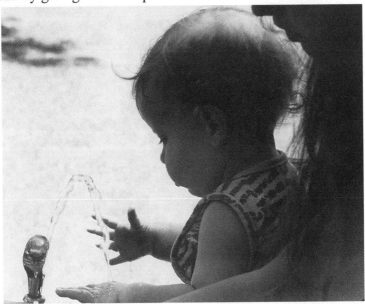

He loves to play in the water.

Making Toys

Rice bags. Make him some small rice bags and show him how to throw them. Use a different textured fabric for each little bag, fur, satin, corduroy, and vinyl, for example. Simply cut two circles of fabric for each rice bag. With right sides together, sew tightly (preferably on a sewing machine) around the edge leaving a one-inch space for turning and stuffing. Turn right side out. Fill with rice. Sew up the hole with tiny stitches.

Using rice to stuff these little bags is far safer than using beans. He could choke on a bean. He could have a real problem if he stuffed a bean in his ear or nose. Don't risk it.

Feel-box. Use a box for the container. Put in a linoleum square, a playing card, big rubber sink stopper, and squares of different kinds of textured fabric.

Coffee can/clothespins toy. You can make a fine toy using a one-pound coffee can and the old-fashioned nonspring clothespins. Make sure the edge of the coffee can is smooth. Simply set the clothespins on the edge of the can. You might want to use a non-toxic paint to paint them red, yellow, and blue. You don't expect him to learn his colors yet, but you begin to introduce the idea of color when you say, "Let's put the red one on the can."

Drop the spool in the hole. A coffee can with a plastic lid can also be used for a "drop the spool in the hole" game. Cut a hole in the plastic coffee can lid a little bigger than the spools. Then show baby how to drop the spools into the can. Lids from frozen juice containers also work well as the drop-in toy.

when they get so small he could choke if he put them in his mouth.

When baby can sit up by himself, you'll probably bathe him in the big bathtub. He'll love having a few floating toys with him. Tell him to wash the fish's hair while you wash his.

A plastic sieve for water play can be made from the lower half of a plastic milk jug. Just poke holes in it with an ice pick.

Make him a bath mitt with a washcloth. Cut two pieces of cloth the shape and size of baby's hand. Sew them together and, if you like, decorate them. Let him help wash himself with his mitten. Of course you'll never turn your back on him for a second while he's in the water.

Your Exciting Challenge

Loving, caring for, and guiding your child throughout her early life is an exciting challenge. Your baby has become a "real" person, a child who is on her way to becoming a self-sufficient individual.

You are an important part of her growth as you love her, care for her, and enjoy games and activities with her.

Enjoy your time together.

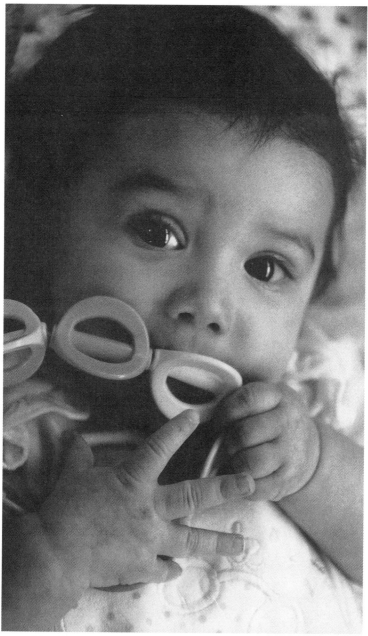

Mom has a wonderful incentive for working toward her goals.

15

Working Toward Your Future

- Continuing School
- Day Care Needed
- If Relatives Can't Help
- Choosing a Caregiver
- Paying for Child Care
- Planning Your Family
- Your Long-Range Goals

It's harder being a single parent although Alice's father has been helping me. But he's too serious. He says within a year we should have this and that, and we'll get married. But I'm not going to marry nobody.

This is what I want to do. I'm going to finish high school in two years, I hope. Then I want to go to nursing school. I don't want to be on welfare. I feel I want to make my own money.

Melanie, 15 - Alice, 13 months

My future plans are to go back to school and get my high school diploma. I need to do this because it's a feeling I just can't shake off.

*It's like an itch that I can't scratch. In other words, I
need to do it for my peace of mind.*

Deborah, 16 - 7 months pregnant

A mother who has her first child before she is 18 is
likely to be poor during much of her life. Many young
mothers have found they must rely on welfare or minimum
wage for survival. Today, however, welfare reform seri-
ously limits the length of time a young mother qualifies for
this help.

A high percentage of the children born to teenage mothers grow up in poverty. However, it doesn't seem to be the
early parenting that causes the poverty. *It's the lack of a
good education and job skills.* That lack, of course, often
goes hand in hand with early motherhood — and
fatherhood.

Most young mothers of 15, or even 17, find it difficult to
continue their education. An obvious reason is the lack of
good and affordable child care in many areas. Even if a
grandmother is available for babysitting during the day, a
teenage mother will find high school life different and
usually harder than it is for her non-parenting friends.

For many young parents, it's too difficult. A majority of
the women in this country who deliver a child before 18
never finish their high school education.

Nearly half of all families headed by women live in
poverty. Women without a high school education are more
likely to head a family than are women who graduated. Yet
these women with less education won't be able to earn as
much as will their better-educated friends.

It seems ironic. If she doesn't have an education, she
can't get a good job and can't earn as much money. Yet she
is more likely to be the sole wage earner for her family.
Life isn't always fair.

Continuing School Is Crucial

Statistics show that if a young mother completes her education and doesn't have additional children right away, she may do as well as her friends who delay childbearing until later. If she becomes pregnant at an early age, gets married, drops out of school, and has more children rather quickly, she's likely to have money problems throughout her life.

These are factors you may be able to control. You start with your own situation. If you are a young parent with a child to support and care for, that's where you start with your life planning.

If you aren't already married, you may decide to postpone your wedding. You may make sure you don't get pregnant again before you think you're ready for another baby. And you can do everything possible to continue your education.

I want to finish school for sure. It will be hard, but I've got to finish. Eventually I want to work with computers, but I'd like to stay home with the baby for awhile. At first I want a part-time job. Then when Racquelle starts school, I'll work full-time.

Cheryl, 15 - Racquelle, 2 months

Day Care Desperately Needed

Most young parents need day care services in order to complete their high school education. Day care isn't available for teenage parents in most school districts in the country.

Finding day care for her child is a serious problem for many young mothers. They need to continue their education, acquire job skills, and work in order to be self-supporting. To do this, they must have day care for their children. The lack of day care services condemns many young parents to reliance on welfare income for survival.

No longer, however, can a single mother depend on even the small welfare grant once available to single mothers who qualified. Welfare reform moved some of the decision-making on this issue to the states. The amount of time an individual qualifies for welfare support is now severely limited. For some teen parents, the challenge of supporting their family is overwhelming, especially if no one else in the family can care for their child.

Some young parents have a mother who is home at least part of the time. Alison's mother works, but is home by early afternoon. She is willing to take care of Stevie when she gets home, so Alison has planned a work schedule which will permit her to be home with her son during much of his waking time:

I'm going to look for a job soon as a hospital ward clerk. I'll try to get swing shift so I can be here most of the day with Stevie. My mother comes home from work by mid-afternoon. She could take care of Stevie when I go to work.

He stays up late, so I could put him to bed when I get home at 10 or 11 p.m. I'd like to be able to do that.

Alison, 18 - Stevie, 2 months

If Relatives Can't Help

Many grandparents, of course, are not available for babysitting. In the first place, they may not want to care for a child. Perhaps your mother feels she has raised her family and she doesn't want to start over again. You can probably understand her feelings.

Even if she's willing to babysit, grandma may have a job herself. Everyone in your family may already be working.

There may be no one at home who will/can take care of your baby for you.

> *I do most of the caregiving. I take her to school because they started a daycare this semester. It's a real help. My mom goes to work, and I didn't know what I was going to do*
>
> Alaina, 17 - Caelin, 4 months

Unless you're one of the lucky few teenage parents in this country whose school offers child care for its students' babies, you have a real problem. You know how important it is to continue your education. Perhaps you've finished high school, but you want to get further job training or go on to college. You may be ready to get a job now, and you don't want to settle for staying home and living on aid even if you might qualify for a short time.

Who will care for your child while you're in school or working?

Some schools have infant care on campus.

Most day care centers are for children who are at least
two years old. Many will only accept children who are
toilet-trained. Your community may not even have a
childcare center which takes babies and toddlers. To find
out, check with your school district and family service
agencies.

Family day care may be available. In this arrangement, a
person cares for a small number of children in her/his own
home. Some day care homes are licensed, some are not.

In order to provide good day care, one person should be
responsible for no more than five children including her/his
own. No more than two of these children should be under
two years of age.

If you can afford it, you might prefer to find a caregiver
who will come to your home to care for your child. Babies
and toddlers aren't likely to want the same schedule as you
must follow. Being able to let your child sleep while you go
on to school could be good for both of you.

Choosing a Caregiver

The decision you make about day care for your child is
extremely important. Yet some people appear to put less
thought into selecting a caregiver for their child than they
do in buying a car! Whether you choose a day care center,
family day care, or a caregiver who comes to your home,
be sure you put a lot of thought into your choice.

Ask questions, lots of them. Don't hire the first person
you find. Talk to several caregivers, then choose the one
you think would be best for your child. One mother
described her search for a caregiver for her small son:

*I started answering other people's ads in our local
paper. Then I ran an ad myself, and that was how I
met the best ones.*

*When people called me, I would ask them a bunch
of questions. I could tell from that first telephone
conversation that I didn't want some of them. I interviewed at least twenty people before I decided.*

I had lots of questions:

- *How many kids do you care for?*
- *How old are they?*
- *How do you discipline children?*
- *What do you do when a baby cries?*
- *When my son starts crawling, how will you pro-
tect your house? What about child-proofing? (If
she said she used a playpen, she was off my list.)*

*If I liked what she said on the phone, I would visit
her, preferably without a lot of advance notice. I
wanted to see what her house was like, how she
coped. If she cared for other kids, I would try to visit
while they were there.*

*Of course I wanted to be sure she had a place for
Bryan to eat, to sleep, to play. What kinds of activities
would she have for toddlers? I asked all sorts of
questions.*

Tricia, 18 - Bryan, 6 months

Remember, you're the employer when you hire a
caregiver. You're the one making the decision. You have
the right to ask about anything that might have something
to do with your child's welfare. Ideally, you'll be able to
find someone who will care for and love your child in
much the same way as you do when you're with him.

Before you make your selection, be sure to ask if the
caregiver takes care of sick children. If she doesn't, perhaps
you have a friend or someone in your family who is willing
to be on call for babysitting during minor illnesses. Babies
and children get sick at inconvenient times.

Her school district provides child care and transportation.

Once you find a caregiver, will you continue checking
on the kind of care your child is receiving? If he isn't
talking yet, he can't tell you what is going on when you're
gone. Even if he's older, you need to know as much as
possible about his "other home." You could make excuses
to visit your child occasionally at unexpected times. This is
one way to learn about the kind of care he's receiving. A
good caregiver should welcome your interest and concern.

Paying for Child Care

Finding child care is one thing. Paying for it is another.
If you qualify for TANF (Temporary Aid for Needy Families), talk to your social worker. There may be extra money
available for child care while you continue your education
or learn job skills. Or you might qualify for a child care
grant through your local college. You can probably find out
by contacting the women's center at the college.

If you're on welfare, perhaps you could get into a program that provides assistance with on-the-job training. Such a program might provide extra help with child care, transportation, and other job-related expenses while you're in school or in job training.

If you can't afford to pay a caregiver, and you have no one who will take care of your child at no charge, can you trade child care duties with another young parent? It would be hard to make such an arrangement work if you need to attend high school full-time. If you're interested in attending night school, or if you're a college student, a trade might work. Schedule your classes so you can care for the other child while her mother is in class. Then she can be responsible for yours while you go to school. Caring for two children while you're trying to study would be difficult. It could be a way, however, to get that education you need so badly for your child's sake as well as your own.

Planning Your Family

I'm going to have two children at the most. I think two is enough. I think ideally I would have another one when Dale's about three when he more or less does things on his own.

Arlene, 17 - Dale, 11 months

Many teen mothers and fathers who have one child are able to continue their education and work toward their goals. If they have a second child before they have finished school, the difficulties multiply. Having more than one child limits one's independence drastically:

It's really hard — a second kid seems like five more. I guess I shouldn't have had her. I tell Charles, "You were right. I should have had an abortion." I wanted to get everything over with — graduate, get

*my license, have the two kids. But now I don't really
have anything. I'm tired and nervous and crabby.*

Colleen 18 - Ruby, 7 months; Hilda, 21 months

The money cost of having a second baby soon after the
first can be overwhelming:

*You don't think the expense of a second baby is
that much, but it is. It costs a lot more with Ruby.
Charles used to work overtime last year for extras like
Christmas. Now he has to work overtime so we can
make it through the month.*

*Maybe it wouldn't be so bad if we were living in a
house and had a lot of things, then said, "We're
broke." But it shouldn't happen when we're in a one-
bedroom apartment. You wouldn't believe what it
costs for these two kids.*

Colleen

From baby's standpoint, waiting three or even four years
before the next child is wise. A two-year-old needs about as
much care, in different ways, as does an infant.

*When we brought Leon home from the hospital,
DeeDee was three. She wanted to hold him, so we set
her down on the couch and propped a pillow on her
so she could. Ever since, he's been her baby. We've
had very little jealousy.*

*If we had had him sooner, DeeDee couldn't have
enjoyed being a baby long enough. I wanted her to be
a little more independent so she would be used to me
not spending so much time with her.*

*A lot of mothers I've seen have their kids real close
together. It kind of makes the oldest child feel ne-
glected. The little baby has to grow up so fast instead
of enjoying being a baby.*

Tamera, 21 - Leon, 10 months; DeeDee, 4 years

Babies do come by accident. If you don't want another child right away, birth control is essential. This could be simply not having intercourse, but most parents will want some other kind of contraceptive. If you're breastfeeding, don't count on it to keep you from getting pregnant. You can get pregnant even though you're breastfeeding.

If you're breastfeeding, check with your doctor about taking the birth control pill. Some pills are likely to cut down on your milk supply. It might be better to choose another contraceptive while you're breastfeeding.

This might be a good time to ask your doctor about inserting an IUD (intrauterine device). Or you might consider the contraceptive implant or the every-three-months Depo-Provera shot. Check with your healthcare provider.

If the man uses a condom (rubber) and the woman uses foam, the two methods together are as successful at preventing conception as is the pill or the IUD. Both the condom and foam can be bought at a drugstore with no prescription from the doctor.

For more information on birth control methods, see *Your Pregnancy and Newborn Journey* by Lindsay and Brunelli.

Sexually active couples need to discuss their thinking concerning contraception. If this is difficult for you, remember that having another baby too soon would also be hard on your partner. Brad talked about this issue:

I'd rather have three years between children. I want my first son to have time for me to teach him.

How to talk about sex? First of all, be alone. Ask her how she feels about using protection. How many kids do you want to have? If one or the other doesn't want to use protection, they have to talk it through.

Brad, 17 - Adam, 13 months

If you aren't pregnant now, and you don't want to have a

child soon, you have two choices. One, of course, is not to have sex. If you're having sex, use birth control — always.

Your Long-Range Goals

Long-range goals are important too. Where do you want to be in five years? The problem with long-range goals, however, is that they're too easy. You might say, "In five years, I'll be out of school, married, and living in a big house. We'll have another baby. Doug will be working, and I'll stay home with the children."

That's a long-range goal, and if this is what you want, by all means continue planning and working toward it.

Most important, what are you doing this year, *this month,* to work toward the life you want for yourself and your child? What must you do in order to continue your education? What steps can you take *now* to begin or continue your job skills training?

If you and your baby's other parent are together, you both need to continue your education and job skills training — unless, of course, one or both of you is job-ready now.

Sometimes young mothers still think they won't have to get a job because their baby's father will support them. For most of us, this is not a realistic expectation for several reasons:

- Many two-parent families find both parents must work to support their family.

- The majority of teenage marriages end in a short time.

- As a parent, you need to be educated in order to be the best possible parent to your child.

What are you doing today to make a satisfying future for yourself and your child?

Appendix

About the Author

Jeanne Warren Lindsay is the author of sixteen books for and about pregnant and parenting teens. Half a million copies of her books had been sold by 1998.

Lindsay's books deal with teenage pregnancy, parenting, adoption from the birthfamily's perspective, and teen relationships. Her *Teen Dads: Rights, Responsibilities and Joys* was selected by the American Library Association as a Recommended Book for Reluctant Young Adult Readers.

Lindsay has worked with hundreds of pregnant and parenting teenagers. She developed the Teen Parent Program at Tracy High School, Cerritos, California,, and coordinated the program for many years. Most of her books are written for pregnant and parenting teens, and quotes from interviewees are frequently used to illustrate concepts.

Lindsay grew up on a farm in Kansas. She has lived in the same house in Buena Park, California, for 36 years. She loves to visit the Middle West, but says she's now addicted to life in southern California. She and her husband, Bob, have five children and five grandchildren.

Lindsay is the editor of *PPT Express*, a quarterly newsletter for teachers and others working with pregnant and parenting teens. She speaks frequently at conferences across the country, but says she is happiest while interviewing young people for her books or writing under the big elm tree in her backyard.

Bibliography

The following bibliography contains books of interest to pregnant and parenting teens. Workbooks and other classroom aids are available for some of these titles. The address and phone number of a publisher is listed only with the first resource described.

Prices quoted are from *Books in Print,* 1997-1998. Because prices change so rapidly, however, and because publishers move, call your local library reference department for an updated price and address before ordering a book. If you can't find a book in your bookstore, you can usually get it directly from the publisher. Enclose $3 for shipping per book. See page 223 for an order form for Morning Glory Press publications.

Brinkley, Ginny, and Sherry Sampson. Illus. by Gail Spratt Cooper. *You and Your New Baby: A Book for Young Mothers.* Also in Spanish—*Usted y su nuevo bebé.* 1991. 80 pp. $4.95. Quantity discounts. Pink Inc! P.O. Box 866, Atlantic Beach, FL 32233-0866. 904/285-9276.
Simple and complete guide for caring for baby. Written in a format for easy understanding.

Eley, Eleanor. **"You and Your Baby: Playing and Learning Together."** **"You and Your Baby: A Special Relationship."** 1994. 35 pp. each. $2.65 each. Bulk discounts. The Corner Health Center, 47 North Huron Street, Ypsilanti, MI 48197. 313/484-3700.
Gorgeous photos of teen parents and their children on every other page. Each booklet contains helpful information at a very easy reading level.

Elliot, Linda K., Gail Breakey, and Linda Fox. Illus. by Sherry Nelson. *A Dance with Your Baby: A Guide to Infant Care and Development.* 1996. 38 pp. $3.40 ppd. Hawaii Family Stress Center, 1833 Kalakaua Avenue, Ste. 1001, Honolulu, HI 96815. 808/947-5700.
A beautiful, simply written booklet for new parents, a guide to promoting strong bonding and attachment between parent and infant.

Green, Martin I. *A Sigh of Relief: The First-Aid Handbook for Childhood Emergencies.* 1994. 384 pp. $16.95. Bantam Books, 414 East Golf Road, Des Plaines, IL 60016. 312/827-1111.
Lots of illustrations and information. Easy-to-find suggestions for treating childhood emergencies. It's a great resource for teen parent classes.

Heine, Arthur J. *Surviving After High School: Overcoming Life's Hurdles.* 1996. 244 pp. $14.95. J-Mart Press. P.O. Box 8884, Virginia Beach, VA 23450-8884. 800/487-4060.
Contains an amazing amount of information about independent living— getting and keeping a job, taxes, budgets, shopping, handling a checking account and credit card, housing, transportation, and much more. Excellent information source for teens highly motivated to live on their own.

Lansky, Vickie. *Feed Me—I'm Yours.* 1994. 130 pp. $9. Meadowbrook, Inc., 18318 Minnetonka Boulevard, Deephaven, MN 55391. 800/338-2232.
An excellent cookbook for new parents. Lots of recipes for making baby food "from scratch." Also includes directions for kitchen crafts.

_____. *Games Babies Play from Birth to Twelve Months.* 1993. 112 pp. $8.95. The Book Peddlers, 15245 Minnetonka Boulevard, Deephaven, MN 55345-1510. 800/255-3379.
Collection of activities — 20-30 ideas for each three months of the first year. Assign several activities each week to students for interacting with their babies as part of your ages and stages curriculum.

Leach, Penelope. *Your Baby and Child from Birth to Age Five.* Revised, 1997. 560 pp. $20. Alfred A. Knopf, 400 Hahn Road, Westminster, MD 21157. 800/733-3000.
An absolutely beautiful book packed with information, many color photos

*and lovely drawings. Comprehensive, authoritative, and outstandingly
sensitive guide to child care and development.*

Lerman, Evelyn. ***Teen Moms: The Pain and the Promise.*** 1997.
192 pp. Paper, $14.95; hardcover, $21.95. Morning Glory Press.
*Teenage mothers talk to us — to the adults surrounding them who can't
decide if these young women are whores, trash to be discarded by society, or
if they are victims of hopelessness and helplessness that poverty spawns.
Stories from teen moms together with illuminating research.*

Lewis, Barbara S. *A Good Beginning: Enjoying Your Baby's First Year.*
1990. 32 pp. $8.98. New Readers Press, Publishing Division of
Laubach Literacy International, P.O. Box 888, Syracuse, NY 13210-
0888. 1-800-448-8878.
*To be hung up like a calendar, it suggests activities for parent and baby for
each month of the first year. Available in English and Spanish.*

Lindsay, Jeanne Warren. *Do I Have a Daddy? A Story About a Single-
Parent Child.* 1991. 48 pp. Paper, $5.95; hardcover, $12.95. Free
study guide. Spanish edition available. Morning Glory Press.
*A beautiful book for the child who has never met his/her father. A special
sixteen-page section offers suggestions to single mothers.*

_____. *School-Age Parents: The Challenge of Three-Generation
Living.* 1990. 224 pp. Paper, $10.95; hardcover, $15.95. Teacher's
Guide/Study Guide, $2.50 set. Morning Glory Press.
*A much needed book for dealing with the frustrations, problems, and
pleasures of three-generation living. Useful for helping teen parents
communicate with **their** parents.*

_____. *Teen Dads: Rights, Responsibilities and Joys.* 1993. 192 pp.
Paper, $9.95; hardcover, $15.95. Teacher's Guide and Workbook,
$2.50 each. Morning Glory Press.
*A how-to-parent book especially for teenage fathers. Offers help in
parenting from conception to age 3 of the child. Many quotes from and
photos of teen fathers.*

_____. *Teenage Couples — Caring, Commitment and Change:
How to Build a Relationship that Lasts. Teenage Couples —
Coping with Reality: Dealing with Money, In-laws, Babies and
Other Details of Daily Life.* 1995. 208, 192 pp. Paper, $9.95 ea.;
hardcover, $15.95 ea. Workbooks and curriculum guide available.
Morning Glory Press.
Series covers such important topics as communication, handling arguments,

keeping romance alive, sex in a relationship, jealousy, alcohol and drug addiction, partner abuse, and divorce, as well as the practical details of living. Lots of quotes from teenage couples.

_____. ***The Challenge of Toddlers.*** 1998. 208 pp. each. Paper, $12.95 each; hardcover, $18.95 each. Morning Glory Press.
How-to-parent books especially for teenage parents. Lots more quotes from teenage parents who share their experiences with their children.

_____ and Jean Brunelli. ***Your Pregnancy and Newborn Journey.*** 1998. 208 pp. Paper, $12.95; hardcover, $18.95; Spanish ed., ***Adolescentes como Padres—Jornada de tu embarazo y nacimiento del bebé.*** 1993, 192 pp. Paper, $9.95; hardcover, $15.95. Morning Glory Press.
Prenatal health book for pregnant teenagers. Includes section on care of the newborn and a chapter for fathers. Also available in Easier Reading Edition (third grade reading level) with workbook and teacher's guide. Same prices. Board games, one with this title and another, "Baby's First Year," provide excellent learning reinforcement.

_____ and Sally McCullough. ***Discipline from Birth to Three.*** 1998. 208 pp. Paper, $12.95; hardcover, $18.95. Morning Glory Press.
Provides teenage parents with guidelines to help prevent discipline problems with children and for dealing with problems when they occur.

Marecek, Mary. ***Breaking Free from Partner Abuse.*** 1993. 96 pp. $7.95. Quantity discount. Morning Glory Press.
Lovely edition illustrated by Jami Moffett. Underlying message is that the reader does not deserve to be hit. Simply written. Can help a young woman escape an abusive relationship.

McCoy, Kathy, and Charles Wibbelsman, M.D. ***The New Teenage Body Book Guide.*** 1992. 288 pp. $15. Berkley Publishing, P.O. Box 506, East Rutherford, NJ 07073. 800/631-8571.
Crammed with information for teenagers about everything from their bodies, changing feelings, teenage beauty, and special medical needs of young adults to sexuality, venereal disease, birth control, pregnancy and parenthood. Lots of quotes from young people, sometimes in the form of questions.

MELD Parenting Materials. Nueva Familia: Six books in Spanish and English. ***Baby Is Here. Feeding Your Child, 5 months-2 years. Healthy Child, Sick Child. Safe Child and Emergencies. Baby Grows. Baby Plays.*** 1992. $10 each. MELD, Suite 507, 123 North

Third Street, Minneapolis, MN 55401. 612/332-7563.
Very easy to read books full of information. Designed especially for Mexican and Mexican American families, but excellent for anyone with limited reading skills. Ask MELD for catalog of other materials designed especially for school-age parents.

Nykiel, Connie. **What It Takes: A Survival Guide for Young and Teen Dads-to-Be.** 1995. 80 pp. $5. For Teen Moms Only, P.O. Box 962, Frankfort, IL 60423-0962. 815/464-5465.
Booklet to help a teen father cope with his new life.

Parent Express Series: *Parent Express: For You and Your Infant. Spanish edition: Noticlas Para Los Padres. Parent Express: For You and Your Toddler.* Each newsletter, 8 pp. $4 each set. ANR Publications, University of California, 6701 San Pablo Avenue, Oakland, CA 94608-1239. 510/642-2431.
Wonderful series of newsletters for parents. The first set, available in English and Spanish, starts two months before delivery and continues monthly through the first year of the child's life. Second set with twelve letters covers second and third years. Good resource for teen parents. Beautiful photos, easy reading.

Pollock, Sudie. **Will the Dollars Stretch?** *Teen Parents Living on Their Own.* 1996. 96 pp. $6.95. Teacher's Guide, $2.50. Morning Glory Press.
Four short stories about teen parents moving out on their own. As students read the stories, they will get the feel of poverty as experienced by many teen parents —as they write checks and balance the checkbooks of the young parents involved.

Renfrew, Mary, Chloe Fisher, and Suzanne Arms. **Bestfeeding: Getting Breastfeeding Right for You.** 1995. 240 pp. $14.95. Celestial Arts Publishing, P.O. Box 7123, Berkeley, CA 94707. 800/841-2665.
Marvelous description, with lots of photographs and drawings (150+) of the importance of breastfeeding, and of how to make the process work. Wonderful resource for teacher. While many students may not want to read the whole book, simply looking at the photos and drawings could be helpful.

Reynolds, Marilyn. **True-to-Life Series from Hamilton High.** *Baby Help. Beyond Dreams. But What About Me? Detour for Emmy. Telling. Too Soon for Jeff.* 1993-1998. 160-256 pp. Paper, $8.95 each; hardcover, $15.95 each. Quantity discounts. Morning Glory.
Wonderfully gripping stories about situations faced by teens. Start with **Detour for Emmy***, award-winning novel about a 15-year-old mother. Students who read one of Reynolds' novels usually ask for more. Topics*

cover partner abuse, acquaintance rape, reluctant teen father, sexual molestation, racism, fatal accident, and school failure.

Silberg, Jackie. **Games to Play with Babies and Games to Play with Toddlers.** 1993. 286 pp. $14.95. Gryphon House, Inc., P.O. Box 207, Beltsville, MD 20704-0207. 800/638-0928.
Silberg divides games for the first two years into three-month segments and also into categories such as Growing and Learning Games, Kitchen Games, and Special Bonding Games.

Stewart, Nancy. **Your Baby from Birth to 18 Months: The Complete Illustrated Guide.** 1997. 192 pp. $15.95. Fisher Books, 4239 W. Ina Road, Suite 101, Tucson, AZ 84741. 520/744-6110.
Provides clear and valid information about caring for the new baby on up to age 18 months. Well illustrated.

Wiggins, Pamela K. **"Why Should I Nurse My Baby?" and Other Questions Mothers Ask About Breast Feeding.** 1996. 58 pp. $5.95. The Learning Curve, 4614 Prospect Avenue, #421, Cleveland, OH 44103. 216/881-5151.
Easy-to-read, yet thorough discussion of breastfeeding. Question and answer format. Also ask about the Babies First pamphlets, same source.

Wilkes, Donald L., and Viola Hamilton-Wilkes. **Teen Guide—Job Search: Ten Easy Steps to Your Future.** 1993. 112 pp. $10.95. JEM/ JOB Educational Materials, P.O. Box 4356, West Covina, CA 91791-0356. 818/308-7642.
Easy reading, lots of illustrations. Simplified, practical, basic approach to job hunting. Excellent for teens beginning their job search —and for those teens who, because of lack of basic skills and/or lack of employed family role models, show little interest in getting a job. Good resource.

Williams, Kelly. **Single Mamahood: Advice and Wisdom for the African American Single Mother.** 1998. 190 pp. $12. Carol Publishing Group, 120 Enterprise Avenue, Secaucus, NJ 07094.
Down-to-earth, sister-to-sister guide. Offers suggestions on how to deal with work, school, child support, discipline, dating again, and more.

Wonderley, Stan. **Learning Activities for Infants and Toddlers.** 1998. 248 pp. $22.95. Blue Bird Publishing,
Simple activities using material commonly found in the home. Can help infants and toddlers develop a wide range of skills.

Index

MORNING GLORY PRESS

6595 San Haroldo Way, Buena Park, CA 90620
714/828-1998; 888/612-8254 — FAX 714/828-2049; 888/327-4362

ORDER FORM — Page 1

Please send me the following: Price   Total

Books, Babies and School-Age Parents

    __ Paper 1-885356-22-6   14.95 _____

    __ Hardcover 1-885356-21-8   21.95 _____

Organizing TAPP: Useful Forms for Teen Parent

    __ ***Programs*** Paper 1-885356-23-4   4.95 _____

Teens Parenting Series:

    Your Pregnancy and Newborn Journey

    __ Paper 1-885356-30-7   12.95 _____

    __ Hardcover 1-885356-29-3   18.95 _____

    __ Workbook 1-885356-31-5   2.50 _____

    __ **Board Game** 1-885356-19-6   29.95 _____

    Your Pregnancy and Newborn Journey —

    Easier Reading Edition (GL3) (1991 edition)

    __ Paper 0-930934-61-x   9.95 _____

    __ Hardcover 0-930934-62-8   15.95 _____

    __ Workbook 0-930934-63-6   2.50 _____

    __ Teacher's Guide 0-930934-68-9   2.50 _____

    Adolescentes como padres (1991 edition)

    __ Paper 0-930934-69-5   9.95 _____

    __ Workbook 0-930934-71-7   2.50 _____

    __ Teacher's Guide 0-930934-72-5   2.50 _____

    Your Baby's First Year

    __ Paper 1-885356-33-1   12.95 _____

    __ Hardcover 1-885356-32-3   18.95 _____

    __ Workbook 1-885356-34-x   2.50 _____

    __ **Video** 51 min. 1-885356-02-1   195.00 _____

    __ **Board Game** 1-885356-20-x   29.95 _____

    Challenge of Toddlers

    __ Paper 1-885356-39-0   12.95 _____

    __ Hardcover 1-885356-38-2   18.95 _____

    __ Workbook 1-885356-40-4   2.50 _____

    Discipline from Birth to Three

    __ Paper 1-885356-36-6   12.95 _____

    __ Hardcover 1-885356-35-8   18.95 _____

    __ Workbook 1-885356-37-4   2.50 _____

    __ **Video** 52 min. 0-930934-97-0   195.00 _____

Teen Dads: Rights, Responsibilities and Joys

    __ Paper 0-930934-78-4   9.95 _____

    __ Hardcover 0-930934-77-6   15.95 _____

    __ Workbook 0-930934-79-2   2.50 _____

    __ Teacher's Guide 0-930934-80-6   2.50 _____

Teens Parenting* Sample Kit** — 5 books (4 ***Teens
    Parenting titles plus ***Teen Dads***),
    5 workbooks, 3 guides,

    __ 2 videos, 2 games   498.00 _____

Quanity Discounts Available on Single, Multiple Titles

Total (Transfer to back page) _____

ORDER FORM — Page 2

			Price	Total

Novels by Marilyn Reynolds:

		Price	Total
— *Baby Help*	1-885356-27-7	8.95	___
— *But What About Me?*	1-885356-10-2	8.95	___
— *Too Soon for Jeff*	0-930934-91-1	8.95	___
— *Detour for Emmy*	0-930934-76-8	8.95	___
— *Telling*	1-885356-03-x	8.95	___
— *Beyond Dreams*	1-885356-00-5	8.95	___

(Hardcover novels, $15.95 each.)

Breaking Free from Partner Abuse

		Price	Total
—	Paper 0-930934-74-1	7.95	___
— *Did My First Mother Love Me?*	Paper 0-930934-84-9	5.95	___
—	Hardcover 0-930934-85-7	12.95	___
— *Do I Have a Daddy?*	Paper 0-930934-44-x	5.95	___
—	Hardcover 0-930934-45-8	12.95	___
— *¿Yo tengo papá?*	Paper 0-930934-82-2	5.95	___
—	Hardcover 0-930934-83-0	12.95	___

Parents, Pregnant Teens, Adoption Option

		Price	Total
—	Paper 0-930934-28-8	8.95	___

Pregnant? Adoption Is an Option.

		Price	Total
—	Paper 1-885356-08-0	11.95	___
—	Hardcover 1-885356-09-9	17.95	___
— *Surviving Teen Pregnancy*	Paper 1-885356-06-4	11.95	___

School-Age Parents: Three-Generation Living

		Price	Total
—	Paper 0-930934-36-9	10.95	___

Teen Moms: The Pain and the Promise

		Price	Total
—	Paper, 1885356-25-0	14.95	___
—	Hardcover 1-885356-24-2	21.95	___

Teenage Couples: Expectations and Reality

		Price	Total
—	Paper 0-930934-98-9	14.95	___
—	Hardcover 0-930934-99-7	21.95	___
— *Caring, Commitment and Change*			
—	Paper 0-930934-93-8	9.95	___
—	Hardcover 0-930934-92-x	15.95	___
— *Coping with Reality*			
—	Paper 0-930934-86-5	9.95	___
—	Hardcover 0-930934-87-3	15.95	___
— *Will the Dollars Stretch?*	Paper 1-885356-12-9	6.95	___
—	Teacher's Guide 1-885356-15-3	2.50	___

TOTAL (Inc. first page) ___

**Please add postage: 10% of total—Min., $3.50;
15%, Outside U.S.**
California residents add 7.75% sales tax ___

TOTAL ___

Ask about quantity discounts, Teacher, Student Guides.
Prepayment requested. School/library purchase orders accepted.
If not satisfied, return in 15 days for refund.

NAME _____ PHONE_____
ADDRESS _____